PUSHING THE ENVELOPE

Airplanes of the Jet Age

PUSHING THE ENVELOPE

Airplanes of the Jet Age

HAROLD RABINOWITZ

MetroBooks

MetroBooks

An Imprint of Friedman/Fairfax Publishers

©2000, 1998 by Michael Friedman Publishing Group, Inc.

Library of Congress Cataloging-in-Publication Data

Rabinowitz, Harold, 1948–
    Pushing the envelope : airplanes of the jet age / Harold Rabinowitz.
        p.   cm.
    Including bibliographical references and index.
    ISBN 1-56799-596-9
    1. Aeronautics—Technological innovations—History. I. Title
TL515.R235   1998
629.13 ' 09—dc21
                                                    98-4132

Editor: Celeste Sollod
Art Director: Kevin Ullrich
Designer: Robert Beards Design, Inc.
Photography Editor: Valerie E. Kennedy
Production Manager: Camille Lee

Color separations by Radstock Repro
Printed in England by Butler & Tanner Limited

10 9 8 7 6 5 4 3 2

For bulk purchases and special sales, please contact:
Friedman/Fairfax Publishers
Attention: Sales Department
15 West 26th Street
New York, NY 10010
212/685-6610 FAX 212/685-1307

Visit our website:
http://www.metrobooks.com

PAGES 12–13: *The Rockwell B-1B, a variable-wing strategic bomber, is one of the most advanced and sophisticated aircraft ever produced.* PAGES 14–15: *The McDonnell Douglas F-15 Eagle is considered the mainstay of the U.S. Air Force fighter fleet.*

DEDICATION

To the memory of
Professor Ralph Behrends
before whose eyes equations danced
and in whose heart great causes sang

ACKNOWLEDGMENTS

I thank my family, my dear wife, Ilana, and my son, Daniel, who get an even bigger thrill from all of this than I do. To my friends and colleagues who have supported my endeavors goes my gratitude, as well as to those avid readers who took the trouble to write and constructively criticize my last two forays. This book is dedicated to the late Professor Ralph Behrends, a physicist of rare insight and righteous soulfulness. He was peerless as a teacher and rock solid as a friend. Along with the entire physics community, for whom he was the reasonable man's voice of reason, I mourn his passing.

J-1103

CONTENTS

A RARE OPPORTUNITY

As one who has enjoyed writing about aviation almost as much as he has enjoyed learning about aviation, the invitation to write this brief book on the story of record-breaking flight came as a rare opportunity I could not pass up. Almost every book on the history of aviation, it has always seemed to me, ends sooner than the author would like. The simple reason for this is that the story of early aviation, which details the lives and travails of the pioneers of flight, is all so compelling that the aviation writer soon discovers there are only a few pages left in the publishing budget for the latter parts of the story. What often happens is that the post–World War II period is covered in very broad strokes, and the reader is left with the impression that not much has happened in the development of aviation and aeronautical science in the second half of the twentieth century. Certainly there are new planes and new records set, but all of that takes place as a result of the normal course of trial-and-error experimentation, right? A wing is fiddled with here, a few extra octane points added to the fuel mixture there, maybe a new alloy cooked up somewhere—and pretty soon aviation becomes a routine matter of simple experimentation and extending the decimal places.

Nothing could be further from the truth.

In point of fact, the same kinds of intuitive leaps and insights in design and the same heroic determination in testing and experimentation that exemplified the early history of flight can be seen in abundance in the history of postwar aviation. No doubt the big business aviation has become and the proliferation of designs and aircraft in the last fifty years have made the solitary spotlight that shone on the pioneers a thing of the past. Progress takes place in quicker succession and there are more players with more sideshows, but the fundamental human urges that send people into the sky or that prompt a designer to work at a drafting table for hours contemplating a fraction-of-an-inch variation in a wing configuration—these have not changed. They are still the motivations that drive the aviation industry (even if it sometimes seems that the industry itself has forgotten).

In this sense, flying shares a psychological foundation stone with mountain climbing. The famous answer to the question "Why climb a mountain?"—"Because it's there."—expresses the idea that the simple challenge of doing what might (only might) be possible is enough motivation to send people up the side of, say, Everest. Climbing enthusiasts tell me, though, that there is something else contained in this witticism that the nonclimbing public just doesn't get. What climbers know that others do not is that once a mountain has been climbed, the desire to climb it remains undiminished in the minds of those of their number who have not yet scaled it. We lowlanders think that once a peak has been conquered, there is no need to conquer it again. Climbers do not think that way—and neither do fliers.

The breaking of a record only encourages others of like temperament to try to break that record—perhaps in a different way, or maybe to push that record a bit more. "Pushing the envelope" is, by this way of thinking, not simply a matter of racking up ever more impressive numbers. It is a matter of technique: how were those numbers achieved, and under what conditions and against what obstacles? That's why the record breakers mentioned in this volume include not only those who established records of speed and distance but also those who flew under unusual conditions; overland record-breaking is not the same as transoceanic record-breaking, transmountain flying, or Arctic aviation. Flying solo is in a class by itself, and so, of course, are flights powered by human beings alone, by solar power, and by wind power alone. Flying a huge transport aircraft is not the same as flying a one-seater autogyro, or a two-seater jet fighter aircraft in a combat theater.

What *is* the same in all these cases is the gut motivation of the people involved, the way they view their work, and the respect they have for the enterprise of challenging the skies and extending humankind's conquest of those skies. One of the most interesting discoveries that I made in the course of conducting research for this book is the profound respect fliers and designers in one flight setting have for those in another. Jet pilots admire gliders; commanders of space shuttles pay homage to peddlers of bicycle-rigged engines that propel human-powered aircraft across the English Channel. To each, the fliers who pushed their individual envelopes are all worthy of the most profound respect and sincere admiration.

LEFT AND PAGES 10–11: Even more remarkable than the stealth of the B-2 Stealth Bomber by Northrop is its incredibly sensitive and responsive control surfaces, which would be impossible to use without the help of computers.

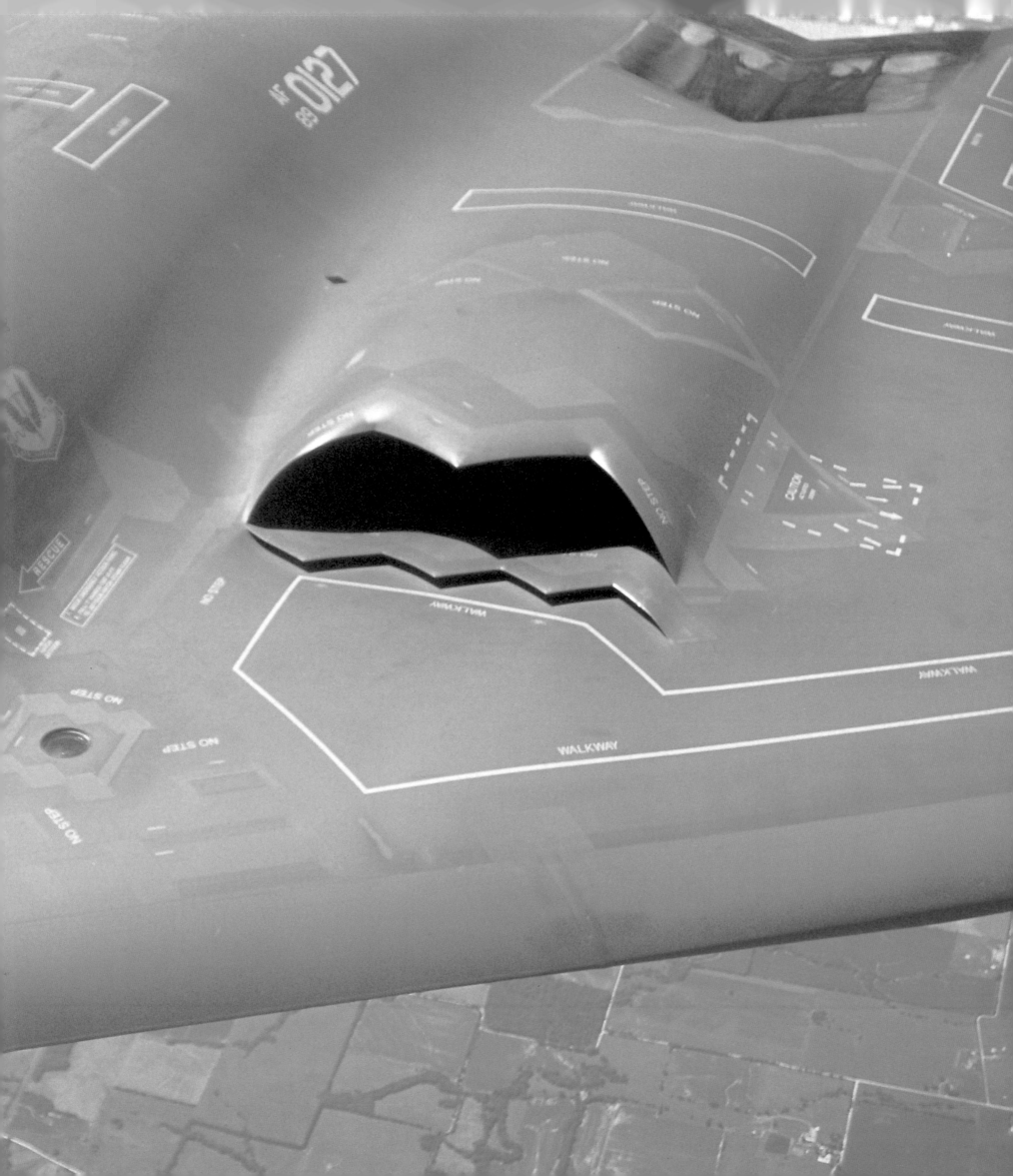

CHAPTER ONE

A BRIEF HISTORY OF ENVELOPE PUSHING

THE STORY GOES THAT AT THE FIRST SUCCESSFUL CREWED FLIGHT OF THE MONTGOLFIER BROTHERS' HOT AIR BALLOON ON NOVEMBER 21, 1783, ONE OF THE SPECTATORS AMONG THE HUNDREDS IN THE GARDENS OF THE CHATEAU LA MUETTE IN THE BOIS DE BOULOGNE WAS NONE OTHER THAN BENJAMIN FRANKLIN, WHO WAS IN FRANCE TO SIGN THE TREATY OF PARIS THAT OFFICIALLY ENDED THE REVOLUTIONARY WAR.

As Jean-François Pilâtre de Rozier and the Marquis François d'Arlandes were carried aloft in the balloon, an aristocrat standing next to Franklin turned to him and said, "What good is that?" Ben is quoted as having replied, "What good is a newborn baby?"

Franklin was not alone in recognizing that great potential was born on that day, and that if humanity could manage to find a way to break the bonds that kept us grounded to the earth, it was only a matter of time before the lifelong dream of being able to fly through the air with the kind of control that birds know would be fulfilled. Once the

LEFT: The Blériot XI in which Louis Blériot made the first airplane crossing of the English Channel in 1909. The intensity of the planning and construction that went into early aircraft is sometimes forgotten because these airplanes seem so fragile and haphazard.

qualms that theologians had about whether it was right for people to fly—and even the Montgolfiers were subject to much vitriol in the French journals about their temerity in contravening the order of nature—were overcome, there was no telling what the inventive human mind could create in the way of flying machines.

Almost from the start of modern aviation, two approaches drove experimenters and builders of aircraft; sometimes these approaches came together, but more often they found it difficult to coexist in one design philosophy. One approach was that flight provided people an opportunity to achieve speeds of movement not possible in any other means of transportation. It was clear from the start that being able to fly through the air would circumvent the forces that retarded speed on the ground: the friction with the ground and the friction of wheels and machinery. The other approach extolled control over speed. The objective was not simply to fly fast, but to maneuver through the sky and feel the sense of ease and command that soaring birds seemed to have. Though the idea that human musculature was not powerful enough to allow for Icaruslike flight by a person equipped with da Vinci-esque wings was firmly established by the nineteenth century, this did not prevent visionaries from wondering how close they could come to this ideal with the machines that were being developed and tested during the century prior to the appearance of the Wright brothers.

This distinction is clear in comparing the approaches of two of the nineteenth-century giants in the field: Hiram Maxim and Otto Lilienthal. Maxim, inventor of

the machine gun and an expatriate American living in England, built experimental machines of size and power—test pilots were lost in the maze of intricate girders, wires, and steam power plants of Maxim's test craft, and Maxim had no interest in experiencing flight himself. In fact, he wasn't even terribly interested in seeing anybody fly; he approached the entire matter as a theoretical problem in engineering and never permitted his aeroplane to fly free of the restraining rails he built as

a test track (even when the craft strained against the rails, trying, it seemed, to break free).

By contrast, Lilienthal's interest was strictly one of control in the air. His designs were aimed at allowing the pilot to conduct maneuvers in flight, and his complex wing designs were directed at sharper turns, figure eights, and lateral and vertical control. Had he not died in 1896, during the last of the more than two thousand glides he made in the foothills of Germany, Lilienthal

By the time this picture of Wilbur Wright at the controls of a Wright Flyer at a demonstration in Auvors, France, was taken, the Wrights had refined the controls from their Kitty Hawk days and had the pilot sitting upright.

would probably have attached a small engine to his glider and been able to lay claim to having been the first to fly, seven years before Kitty Hawk.

Flight was first achieved on the sand dunes at Kitty Hawk, North Carolina, when two brothers, Wilbur and Orville Wright, brought a whirlwind four years of experimentation to a successful close on December 17, 1903. They had gone far beyond Lilienthal and all other pioneers by combining a visionary conceptual ability with an eminently practical scientific approach. Their achievement was well in advance of all competitors around the word, but once they had pointed the way, many others followed.

In the United States, the most important of these followers was Glenn Curtiss, whose knowledge of engines and experience with Alexander Graham Bell's Aerial Experiment Association made him a formidable competitor.

The desire of the Wrights to protect their patents from infringement led to a long and bitter legal struggle with Curtiss and other manufacturers. This was unfortunate, because it detracted from aviation progress in the United States. Ultimately Curtiss proved to be the better businessman, and the Curtiss Aeroplane and Engine Company eclipsed the efforts of the Wrights.

RECORD BREAKING TO THE END OF WORLD WAR I

Almost from the very beginning of the history of flight in the twentieth century, records were kept and (as the saying goes) meant to be broken. The body that became the first record keeper for the world of aviation, and that became the internationally accepted arbiter and standards setter, was the Fédération Aéronautique Internationale (International Aeronautical Federation, or the FAI), founded in Paris in 1905 for the purpose of issuing pilot's licenses. The FAI's main focus in its early years was establishing rules for aerial meets and races; standards for record keeping grew naturally out of that function. The first aviation record recognized by the FAI was a speed record: Alberto Santos-Dumont's attaining a speed of 25.06 mph (40.3kph) in a flight at Bagatelle, France, in 1906. Santos-Dumont also claimed the FAI's

first distance record of 25.8 feet (7.8m) in that same flight. The FAI did not start keeping altitude records until 1908, when Wilbur Wright flew an astonishing 82 feet (25m) high in his *No. 2* biplane.

The FAI has prided itself on being a truly impartial arbiter and regulator of aviation, which of course means it has been no stranger to controversy and charges of favoritism. For the most part, the organization has bent over backward to maintain its integrity and impartiality, a reputation that served it well in sorting out all the claims made during the period of the Schneider trophy races. But the fact that the first FAI altitude record is shared by Wilbur Wright and Frenchman Henri Farman, who was flying a Voisin biplane—both flew to an altitude of 82 feet (25m) on the same day, November 13, 1908—was not a case of getting off on the right foot. In fairness, almost never again was there a similar lapse in the organization's reliability as a record keeper.

OPPOSITE, TOP: In 1907, Alberto Santos-Dumont used Hargraves' box-kite design simply to become airborne. OPPOSITE, BOTTOM: Glenn Curtiss deftly handles the well-engineered controls of his Golden Flyer in 1909. LEFT: In 1909, Hubert Latham attempted a dash over the English Channel in his Antoinette IV, a sleek aircraft designed for speed.

ABOVE: Latham sits at the complicated controls of the Antoinette IV. BELOW: The historic collaboration between Henri Farman (left) and Gabriel Voisin represented the marriage of two flight philosophies—control and speed. OPPOSITE, TOP: One result of the partnership between control and speed was the agile yet quick Farman III, shown winning the 1910 Paris-to-Brussels race. OPPOSITE, BOTTOM: Compare the sophisticated design of the Farman III aircraft with the Blériot XII of just a year earlier.

The year 1909 provided many opportunities for the setting of records. First, Alfred Harmsworth, the publisher of London's *Daily Mail*, offered a prize of £1,000 to the first pilot of any nationality who flew an aeroplane across the English Channel. His intention was to encourage British aviation, at the time lagging behind the French. (It was also behind American aviation, though how badly would not be known until later in the year. It was the first of many such prizes offered by the newspaper baron, who discovered they were good for circulation.) The playing field for this prize was not entirely level, since the flier who then seemed to have the best chance at winning was British aviator Hubert Latham, who had already set distance records greater than the distance required to cross the channel. Prevailing winds favored a west-to-east crossing, which made having a base in England advantageous, and the cliffs of Dover were, in those early days of flight, a barrier any flier crossing the channel had to take seriously.

Latham did, in fact, attempt the crossing first, but his *Antoinette IV* monoplane went down at sea. While Latham prepared the plane for another try (a bit cavalierly, as it turned out), a dark horse candidate, Louis Blériot, a flier and manufacturer who had shown little promise, made a mad dash in his *Blériot XI* monoplane and managed a rocky landing in Northfall Meadow, near Dover Castle.

The second major aviation event of 1909 was La Grande Semaine d'Aviation de la Champagne (Grand Aviation Meeting) at Rheims in August. The event not only ignited public interest in aviation around the world but also established a number of records and, in fact, set the tone for aviation record breaking for years to come. Three records were set at Rheims in the space of a few days, and though these records would soon fall, the importance of speed over agility became firmly established. The three big winners at Rheims were Henri Farman, who established a distance record of 112 miles (180.2km) in his *Farman III*; Glenn Curtiss, who took the coveted speed prize by flying his *Golden Flyer* at 46.6 mph (74.9kph); and Hubert Latham, who took the altitude prize with 508 feet (154.8m). Even Blériot distinguished himself by setting a short-sprint speed record in a noncontest event by flying his *No. XII* at 47.8 mph (76.9kph).

In the years immediately preceding World War I, according to FAI records, the majority of fliers applying for pilot's licenses (called aviator's certificates) were

French—more than one-third of the roughly twenty-five hundred granted—reflecting the great increase in aeronautical development in France during this period. The French were quick to adopt controlled surfaces, such as ailerons, invented by Farman, over the Wrights' cumbersome "wing-warping" system of control; to come to the conclusion that a tractor engine configuration—the propellers in front of the plane—was preferable to a pusher system; and to see the monoplane as the most efficient wing design, though they realized biplanes and triplanes would be necessary until stronger engines came along. Although the internal combustion engine had originated in Germany and had seen its greatest development there and in England and America, the French were most adept at applying a wide variety of engine designs to the airplane.

Not surprisingly, then, in the FAI record books between the Rheims meeting and the suspension of record keeping by the FAI during the war in 1914, most of the speed, distance, and altitude records were held by Frenchmen: Jules Vérdrines and Maurice Prévost, flying Deperdussin monoplanes, established ten consecutive speed records between January 1912 and September 1913, the last being at 126.67 mph (203.8kph). Distance records during this period were vied for by planes flown or built by Blériot, Henri Farman, and Léon Levavasseur, as each held the record several times until Georges Fourny closed the prewar books with a flight of 628 miles (1,010.4km) in a Farman on September 11, 1912. Altitude records were the only area where American aircraft (usually Wright-licensed planes produced by the Short brothers in England) had some standing. These records were held at different times by legendary fliers like Latham, Lincoln Beachy, Léon Morane, Roland Garros, and Georges Legagneaux, who first broke the 20,000-foot (6,096m) barrier on December 29, 1913, in a Nieuport monoplane.

As war approached Europe, governments on the Continent and the British government turned their attention to the possible military applications of aviation. In order for that sort of development to take place as efficiently as possible, the flying of aircraft had to be separated from the design, and more and more aircraft builders relegated the flying to professional pilots and the designing to trained designers. In France, for example, Blériot ceased flying, turning over piloting to the gifted aviator Adolphe Pégoud, while Blériot himself

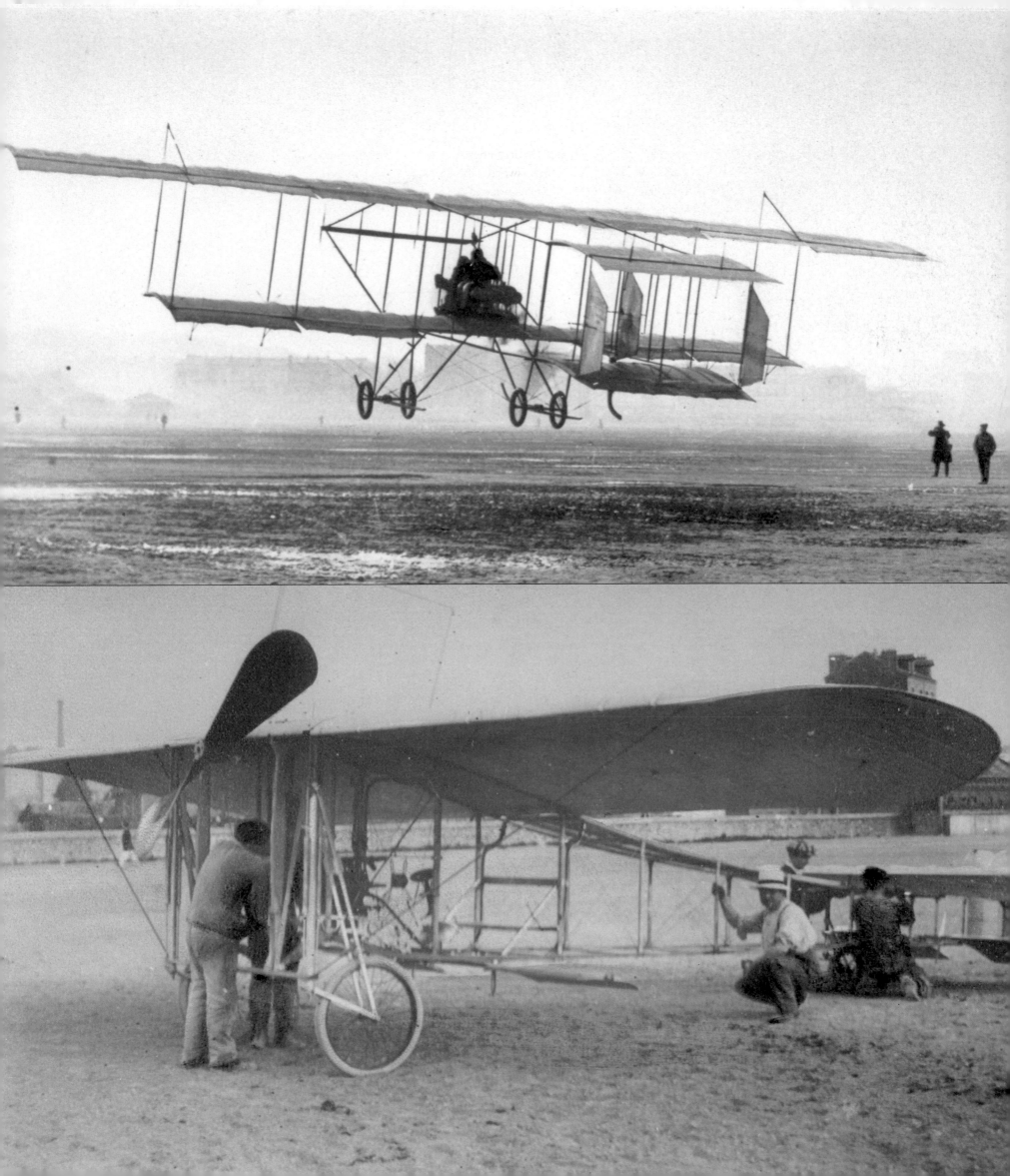

concentrated on the business and design aspects of his manufacturing company. Lone aviators who both designed and flew their planes became increasingly rare (Tom Sopwith is a notable exception in this period.) While Calbraith Rodgers captured the American imagination by flying across the United States in fifty days in the *Vin Fiz Flyer*, Europeans were unimpressed. The many crashes that Rodgers experienced along the way (plus the fact that he missed the goal of thirty days, for which William Randolph Hearst had offered

$50,000) made his feat of dubious military interest. Of greater interest were the pioneering flights of Roland Garros, who flew the first nonstop crossing of the Mediterranean in September 1913, and Georges Chavez's remarkable crossing of the Alps in a Blériot monoplane in 1910. Pégoud had demonstrated the viability of parachuting out of an airplane in August 1913 (answering the question on every pilot's mind: what happens when the plane fails or is hit by artillery fire?).

The war clouds looming on the horizon gave European aviation a greater sense of urgency than American efforts. ABOVE: America's first aviation meet, in 1910, featured crowd-pleasing airships. RIGHT: The first air trip across America was used to sell a grape-flavored soft drink.

The Los Angeles Air Show of January 1910 featured the stunt flying of Lincoln Beachy; the airmanship displayed at Britain's Hendon races, beginning in April 1912, displayed a more serious purpose, as races and specific piloting skills that might have some application in combat were tested and rewarded. The entire business of flying took on a more serious and determined tone in Europe than in America, so not surprisingly the record books were owned by European fliers.

With the advent of World War I, aircraft production took a turn toward agility and engineering and aerial reconnaissance was to be an important factor in the theater of battle for both Allied and Axis forces. The exploits of the celebrated pilots made for wonderful news copy and morale boosters and World War I saw a new kind of record enter the books: the number of kills racked up by the flying aces. Shooting down a plane from a plane was no easy feat—a fact sometimes lost on the video arcade generation. That some fliers managed to down scores of planes in the course of battle was a tes-

tament to flier and machine alike; it is understandable why these pilots were lionized on both sides.

The heroes that emerged from the war—Manfred von Richthofen and Ernst Udet of Germany; René Fonck, Georges Guynemer, and Charles Nungesser of France; Edward Mannock and Billy Bishop of Great Britain; and Eddie Rickenbacker and Frank Luke of the United States—demonstrated the possibility of using air power effectively to protect naval vessels and artillery emplacements, to provide reconnaissance on ground troop movements, and to bomb important targets. Aircraft of sufficient size to allow for serious bombing of targets had not yet been developed, though Germany, Great Britain, and Russia were, at the close of the war, all working on the problem such aircraft posed.

With the development of bomber-size aircraft, yet another parameter was added to the flight characteristics that envelope pushers would be seeking to challenge: size. Igor Sikorsky in Russia had built a fleet of large bombers, some of which were deployed toward the end

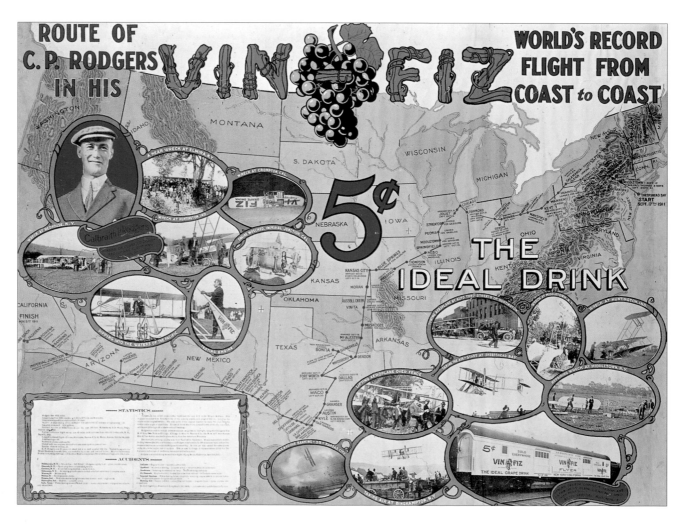

European aviators approached their work with a seriousness born of the tense political climate. LEFT: Roland Garros, destined to become one of France's most celebrated and decorated aviators, had started preparing for his future role as early as 1911. BELOW: Maurice Prévost won the 1913 Schneider Cup in his Deperdussin, honing skills that might be put to military use.

ABOVE: The Vickers Vimy ended its 1919 trans-Atlantic flight nose down in an Irish bog—not as a result of a crash, but because the pilots had jettisoned the front wheel assembly after takeoff to lighten the aircraft. RIGHT: Meanwhile, the Americans were taking things a bit more methodically: engineers prepare one of three Curtiss flying boats, NC-4, in May 1919 in preparation for a trans-Atlantic crossing.

of the war, Germany had a series of heavy bombers in service as early as 1917, and England had aircraft going into production as the war ended. After the armistice, designers and manufacturers in all nations tried to extend the boundaries of flight with respect to speed, distance, size, and maneuverability, knowing full well that these qualities were going to be critical if the world ever again found itself in a global conflict.

BETWEEN THE WARS

The state of aviation after World War I was dreary on both sides of the Atlantic. Europe lay in ruins, and the human cost of the war—even for the United States, which entered late in the conflict—was so high that governments shied away from further developing military aviation. Some of the larger planes that were built toward the end of the war in anticipation of developing a bombing capability but were never used were adapted to long-range flying. The Atlantic was crossed: first by an American flying boat, a Curtiss NC-4, commanded by A.C. Read in May 1919, which put down several times at sea en route from Rockaway, New York, to Portsmouth, England; and then by English fliers John

Alcock and Arthur Whitten Brown, flying a Vickers Vimy bomber nonstop from Newfoundland to Clifden, Ireland, in June of the same year, establishing a distance record of 1,936 miles (3,115km) in the process.

With governments cutting back drastically on development programs in aviation, the field fell to the only other quarters who could apply their talents to flight without government support: amateur flying enthusiasts, who could acquire war surplus aircraft cheaply and tinker with them to their hearts' delight in garages and airfields (which also served as cow pastures), and scientists, who could pursue aeronautical research within the confines of a university research laboratory and could avail themselves of the comparatively inexpensive research tools of paper and pencil to solve problems in aviation.

Both forces played a role in the development of aviation between the wars, and although the early 1920s is often considered a fallow period in aeronautical development, it was, in fact, a period when a great deal of experimentation and innovation was going on that would pay dividends later. Institutes of aeronautical research grew in the United States under the aegis of the National Advisory Committee for Aeronautics (NACA, which became NASA) and under the guidance of Hungarian-

ABOVE, TOP: The pared-down cockpit of Alcock and Brown's Vickers Vimy provided all that was needed to navigate across the Atlantic—a compass. Compare this cockpit with that of the de Havilland DH-60 Moth on page 30. ABOVE, BOTTOM: Alcock and Brown themselves took numerous risks to achieve their goal.

born aerodynamicist Theodore von Karman; in Germany at the University of Gottingen, under the direction of Ludwig Prandtl and later under Alexander Lippisch; and in England under the guidance of B. Melville Jones, Geoffrey Hill, and Frederick Handley Page. These theoreticians studied the complex physical processes that took place when air flowed past a wide variety of wings. Their discoveries resulted in the development of many new wing types; the introduction of devices like slots, flaps, and slats, which would assist the aircraft in different phases of flight (providing more lift on takeoffs and landings, and maintaining a steady airflow across the wing when flying at a steep angle); and progress in the creation of fuselages that were sturdy enough to remain intact while aloft yet light enough to fly.

The contribution that the amateur fliers of the 1920s made to the advance of aeronautics is a bit more difficult to pinpoint. The general collapse of the industry after the war drove most workers and engineers into other fields (in large numbers into the booming auto industry). With money in short supply, the only planes that private individuals were interested in were planes that were cheap to buy and cheap to run. Designers took another look at the spindly creation of Alberto Santos-Dumont before the war and produced a series of planes that bore the imprint of the redoubtable Brazilian (by then in quiet retirement in his native country). Planes like the de Havilland DH 53 Hummingbird, Henri Mignet's Pou-de-Ciel ("Flying Flea"), the Hawker Cygnet (the first plane designed for Hawker by the legendary Sydney Camm), and finally the de Havilland Moth brought to sports flying the most advanced concepts available from the war experience and from contemporary research simply because that was the only way to create a plane the public could afford.

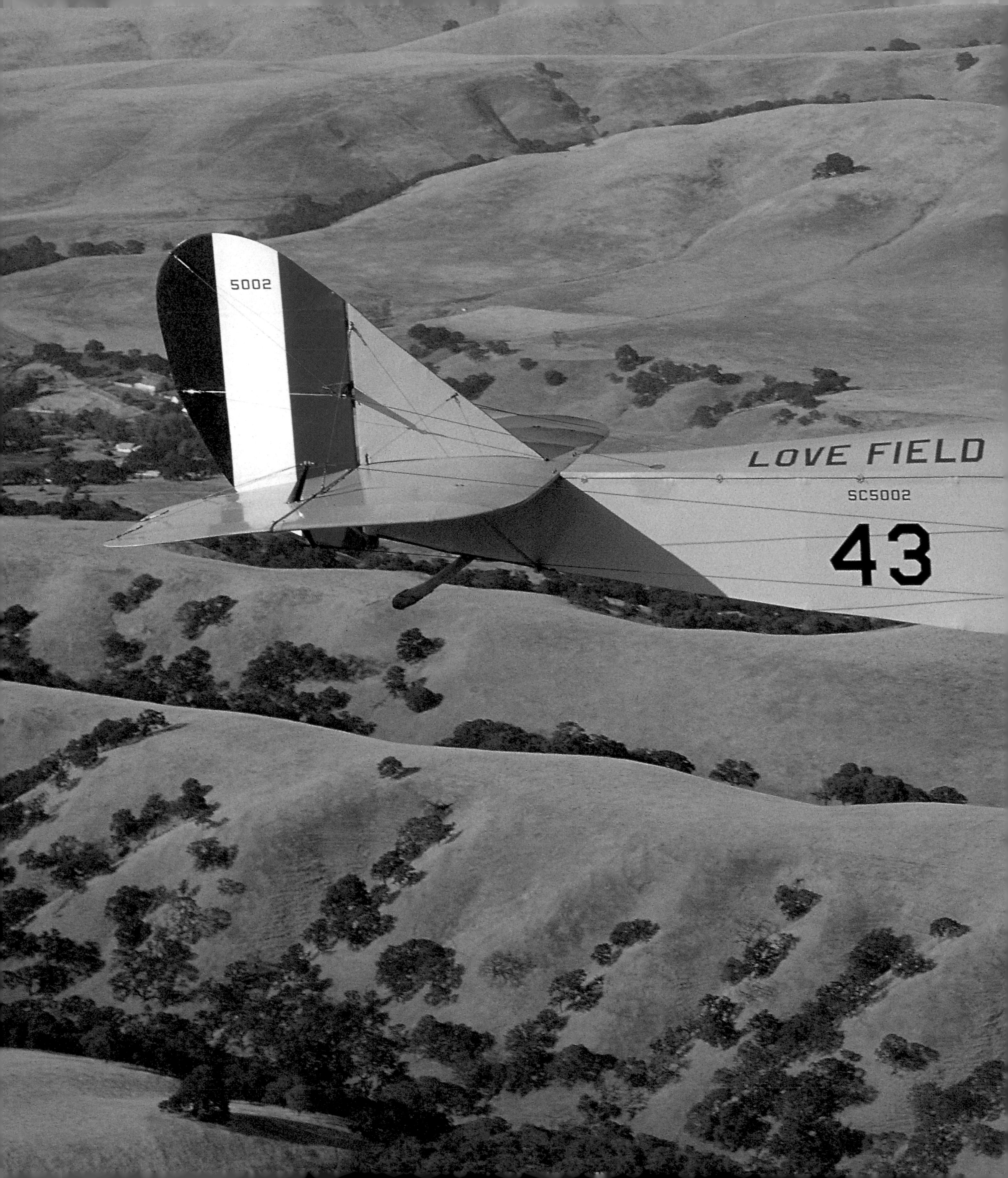
5002
LOVE FIELD
SC5002
43

ABOVE: The death of Harry Hawker in a 1921 plane crash ranks among the greatest tragedies in the history of early aviation. With his untimely death, the aviation industry lost an outstanding and innovative designer. BELOW: The Macchi MC-67 was the Italian entry in the 1929 Schneider Cup. Though the Italians did not win another Schneider trophy, their 1926 win kept them among the leaders in aeronautical science for the next two decades. PAGES 32–33: The Curtiss JN two-seater biplane, the Jenny, combined features of Curtiss' J two-seater land-based trainer with the similar N to produce the JN. The result proved one of the most versatile and widely used aircraft of World War I.

During World War I, Dr. Hugo Junkers had pioneered the development of all-metal monoplanes, including the J 1 and J 2. While technically superior in construction, they were underpowered and only a few were built. They led, however, to the Junkers J 1 armored biplane that was used for ground attack work with great success. After the war, a succession of Junkers designs led to such famous aircraft as the Junkers Ju 52/3m and Ju 88. Many other manufacturers, including Short and Rohrbach, experimented with metal construction. These efforts, combined with advances in aerodynamics such as monocoque construction, cantilever wings, retractable landing gear and controllable pitch propellers, led directly to the modern all-metal aircraft of today.

Metal aircraft development was relatively slow because it required new tooling and was thus expensive in the post-World War I era, when many manufacturers had built large companies based on the production of wood and fabric aircraft. The advantages of metal construction—strength, durability, resistance to weather and so on—were so great that almost all manufacturers adopted the practice.

Advances in aircraft design took time simply because they were paced by the development of more advanced engines, and engines took far more time to design, build, test, and produce than did airframes. Until the advent of the jet age, many of the newest aircraft were "underpowered" in that the airframe could always benefit from the installation of a more powerful engine. A sad example is the famous Dornier Do-X, the twelve-engine flying boat that was so chronically underpowered that it was an economic and technological disaster. In sharp contrast to the ill-fated Do-X, other more reasonably sized Dornier flying boat designs were flown with great success.

Engine development was therefore highly specialized, and experimental engines were found in the high-speed racing planes of the period. The Schneider Cup races were particularly important in this regard, as each nation competed to provide the most powerful engines possible. The effects were great and far-reaching on airframe design, the development of fuels and oils, the improvement of cooling systems, and for setting the requirements for future fighter aircraft. The Supermarine Spitfire and the Rolls-Royce Merlin engine were both products of this process of refinement, and it may be said that winning the Battle of Britain began with the Schneider Cup races.

The air races of the twenties were an important proving ground for aircraft, and records were broken almost daily. The most important of these races were the competitions for the Schneider Cup, a series of air races held twelve times between 1913 and 1931. The provisions of the race were the products of some odd ideas about the likely future of aviation held by the race's founder and benefactor, French arms manufacturer Jacques Schneider, but the competition challenged the best aviation designing teams from Britain, Italy, France, and the United States, the key aviation manufacturers at the time. (Germany was not yet a major air power as a result of restrictions placed by the Treaty of Versailles.) One provision of the race was that the trophy would be won permanently—and the races would end—if a country won

three successive times. Italy did, in fact, win three successive times (1919, 1920, and 1921), but its 1919 victory was invalidated because of rules infractions. The United States came close to retiring the trophy after winning in 1923 and 1925 (no race was held in 1924), but a heroic effort by Italian aviator Mario de Bernardi helped his country capture the trophy in 1926. The British retired the Schneider Cup after victories in 1927, 1929, and 1931, thanks largely to the designs of R.J. Mitchell of the Supermarine S.6. The fact that the air speed record for the years of the Schneider competitions was set either during each race or by the winner in trials shortly afterward is the clearest indication of how important the Schneider Cup competition was to record-breaking aviation. In 1931, the world air speed record was held by

The 1931 Supermarine Schneider Cup team featured three S.6B aircraft. One result of the Schneider Cup races was the professionalization of aeronautical design: every element of the aircraft became the focus of a different engineering group.

G.H. Stainforth flying a Supermarine S.6B at 407 mph (654.8kph). This record was broken three years later by Francesco Agello, who flew an adaptation of the Macchi M.52, the Italian Schneider entrant that had won the 1926 race. Agello's record of 440.7 mph (709kph), attained in a Macchi M.C.72 in October 1934, still stands for piston-engined seaplanes, a further indication of how important the Schneider races had been.

It was at this point in aviation development that fliers started talking about a "sound barrier," a purely theoretical concept which aerodynamicists had been toying with for at least a decade. More about just exactly what was (and was not) meant by this term appears in the next chapter, but it is noteworthy that many designers believed that the speed and altitude limits were close to being reached with the foreseeable technology of aircraft design and propeller-based thrust. With a war looming on the horizon, the aircraft manufacturers looked for improvements in the many other performance parameters that would be vital in air combat-maneuverability (itself a term that includes many independent flight characteristics), range and fuel efficiency, armament, resistance to ground fire, adaptability to ground support, and so on—which created an entirely new set of envelopes for fliers and designers to push (see chapter 4).

Two other areas of achievement characterized the interwar years in the field of aviation: the establishment of the early records in distance flying, and the aeronautical exploration of the polar regions, a kind of flying that confronts the aviator with an entirely unique and severe set of demands.

The period between the wars is aptly called flight's "golden age." Public fascination rose to an all-time high as records were constantly being broken and, in some tragic instances, fliers were killed or disappeared in attempts to become part of history. The importance of the long-distance flights can be discerned from the other name given to the enterprise: route proving. From the start, fliers traversing great distances understood their exploits as laying the foundation for later flights being made routinely over the same route by ordinary travelers. It is only by looking at the distance flights in this context that one may appreciate the intensity of the acclaim and celebrity achieved by Charles Lindbergh when he flew solo across the Atlantic Ocean on May 20–21, 1927. Lindbergh's flight had great impact upon the world of aviation for many reasons. First of all was his charisma and charm, so perfect for a new hero. He handled himself with dignity, and dedicated his efforts to improving aviation. His flight came at a time when aviation had been preparing itself for expansion in a number of ways. The war surplus aircraft which had stifled aviation production in the years after World War I were no longer readily available. The Wright Whirlwind radial engine, used on Lindbergh's plane, had revolutionized the industry, which had been dependent so long on the Curtiss OX-5 and Liberty engines. Almost equally important, the country was in the midst of a stock market boom, so that capital was available to new manufacturers.

Lindbergh's distance record of 3,610 miles (5,806.8km) nonstop stood for about two weeks. Clarence Chamberlain and Charles Levine flew a Bellanca monoplane from New York to Germany on June 4–6, and quite a few other flights captured the world's imagination and established new records in the years between Lindbergh's flight and the mid-1930s. U.S. Army lieutenants Albert F. Hegenberger and Lester J. Maitland made the first U.S.-to-Hawaii nonstop flight in a Fokker C-2 trimotor in June 1927; in many ways, this was a greater feat than Lindbergh's (Hawaii is much easier to miss than Europe), but the prospect of actual commercial flights to the Hawaiian Islands was still clearly

No feat of envelope-pushing can compare with Lindbergh's crossing of the Atlantic for sheer drama and heroism. BELOW: The pilot poses, a bit uncertain, it seems, with his famous aircraft several weeks before his historic flight. OPPOSITE: Crowds gather to watch Charles Lindbergh fly the Spirit of St. Louis. To promote interest in aeronautics, Lindbergh flew the plane throughout North, Central, and South America, finally donating it to the Smithsonian Institution.

failure—made a hero of Commander Richard E. Byrd, who crossed the Arctic, with Floyd Bennett, in a Fokker F.VIIA in May 1926 and the South Pole in a Ford trimotor 4-AT in November 1929.

Probably the most celebrated long-distance flying achievement of the period was the event known as the MacRobertson Race of 1934, the first intercontinental air race. Named after its sponsor, Australian businessman Sir MacPherson Robertson, only nine of the twenty aircraft that began the race between Mildenhall, England, and Melbourne, Australia, finished. The race's favorites, James Mollison and Amy Johnson Mollison, flying one of three de Havilland Comets entered in the race, put down in Karachi with engine trouble and lost the sizable lead they had accumulated. The race was won by C.W.A. Scott and T. Campbell-Black (also flying a Comet), but the big surprise was the second-place winner, a commercial aircraft, a KLM DC-2 that had very few special outfittings for the flight. This was a prime case of course proving and course flying accomplished simultaneously.

WORLD WAR II

That the Second World War was an air war is a truism. What is not often appreciated is that the pressure of war and the needs of the battlefield often forced pilots and air commanders to make do—and perform amazing feats—with aircraft that were not at the cutting edge in performance. Thus, the celebrated Flying Tigers used an aircraft, the Curtiss P-40 Warhawk, that was clearly inferior to Japanese aircraft then in the air and even to other British and American planes in service. The German Ju-87 Stuka was a feared and effective air-support tool in the Blitzkrieg, but its performance parameters were inferior to most, if not all, military aircraft then in production. And the British hailed the Hawker Hurricane for its heroic role in winning the Battle of Britain, but the aircraft was outclassed by Britain's own Supermarine Spitfire, too few of which were available for the momentous air battle, and by several American fighters then being produced. But the exigencies of war and the particular needs of the battlefield made legends of certain aircraft and of particular fliers. In the end, the air battle was resolved by the sheer numbers of planes that the Allies were able to manufacture—a feat that ranks with any military exploits that have been celebrated. In most cases, aircraft were produced without clear notions of how they would perform or without proper testing.

ABOVE: Commander Richard E. Byrd (right) and his co-pilot, Floyd Bennett, get set for their historic flight over the North Pole in May 1926. The pair arrived in London later that same month. OPPOSITE: The Curtiss P-40 (top) was effective in the early stages of the war, but in time, fighters with much improved performance, like the Spitfire (bottom), controlled the skies.

a ways off, so the feat was not celebrated with the same hoopla. The same may be said for the other Pacific crossings of the era. The flights of Charles Kingsford Smith—across the Pacific, Oakland to Brisbane in June 1928, and back the other way in October-November 1934—are among the most amazing yet unheralded in aviation.

The crossing of the polar regions—a trek made difficult by the cold, the lack of navigational landmarks (even compass readings can be tricky so close to the magnetic poles), and the very high risk of freezing to death if forced to make an emergency landing in the event of

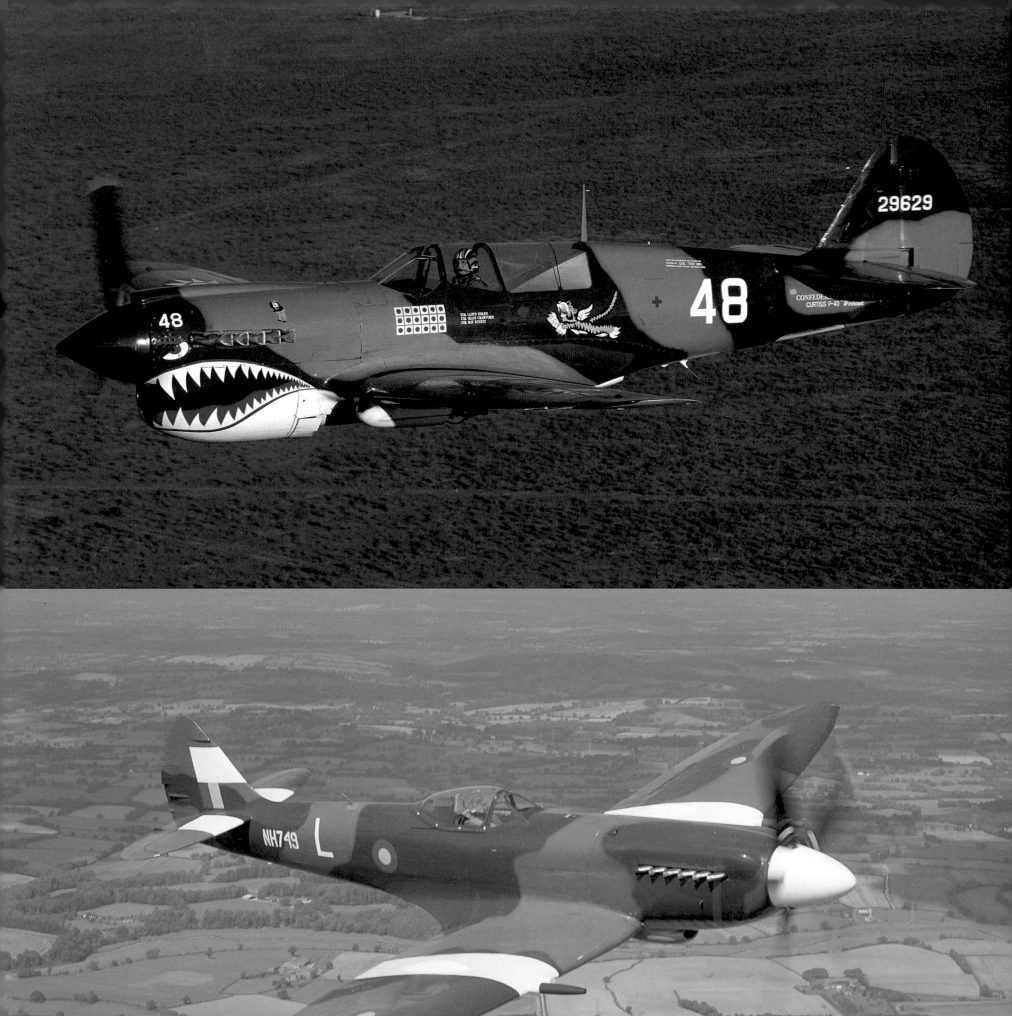

There was a lot of guesswork engaged in by the high commands on both sides, and there are probably a dozen or so decisions that may have affected the outcome of the war.

Of the many outstanding fighter planes produced during the war, the North American P-51 Mustang is considered to be one of the very best.

North American Aviation had responded to a request by the British Purchasing Commission to build Curtiss P-40s under license with a counter offer—an aircraft of original design, guaranteed to be superior to the P-40.

The original P-51 design was powered by the Allison V-1710 engine, and while its performance was superior to that of the P-40, it lacked the high altitude performance necessary for combat in the European theater. A decision was made to adapt the airframe to the Rolls-Royce Merlin engine. The combination proved to be extremely successful, and the Mustang became an effective high altitude fighter, suitable for long-range escort duties. The Mustang was provided to many other Allied air forces, and went on to distinguish itself as a fighter-bomber during the Korean War. Today, there are still about 150 Mustangs flying of the 15,586 built.

OPPOSITE AND PAGES 42–43: For many, propeller-driven aircraft reached its optimum in the P-51 Mustang. BELOW: The key to the outstanding performance of the Mustang must surely have been North American Aviation's painstaking testing program, in which every aspect of aerodynamic design was dissected and evaluated.

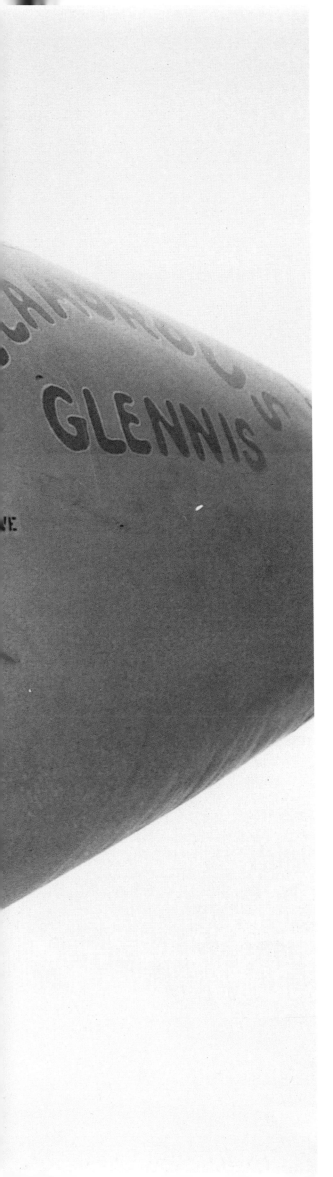

CHAPTER TWO

THE JET AGE

BEFORE LOOKING INTO THE SPECIAL AERODYNAMIC PROBLEMS ENCOUNTERED IN THE P-51 MUSTANG AND HOW THEY LED TO THE BREAKING OF THE SOUND BARRIER, CONSIDER THE QUESTION OF PROPULSION.

Getting an aircraft to fly faster than the speed of sound requires a propulsion system that can generate a great deal of thrust. Looking at the development of power plants in the first two or three decades of flight, it seemed reasonable to assume that prop-driven engines would stay ahead of airplane design and that an engine would be available to power an advanced airplane when the need arose. This is not very surprising when one realizes that, unlike airplanes that need to be tested in wind tunnels or in flight, engines can be "bench tested" in a laboratory. Also, engines have a wide range of industrial applications, so their development often takes place independent of aviation needs.

By the 1940s, laboratory technicians believed they already knew the limit of the effectiveness of a propeller: the speed of sound, which varies according to the temperature of the air. The speed of sound is 661.48 mph (1,064.3kph) in air that is 59°F (15°C), drops to 602 mph (968.6kph) at -30°F (-34°C), the temperature at which most flight takes place; and drops even further to 573 mph (921.9kph) at -69°F (-56°C), the temperature at which high-altitude flight takes place. The ceiling for propeller-driven aircraft was thought to be lower than these speeds because of the unhappy things that occur (aeronautically speaking) when an airfoil approaches the speed of sound. And a propeller is nothing but an airfoil rotating in a plane perpendicular to the direction of flight. The combination of the rotation of the propeller and the forward motion of the aircraft brought the propeller close to the speed of sound well before the aircraft itself ever arrived there. The thrust provided by the propeller as measured in wind tunnel tests plummeted as the speed of the blade approached the speed of sound. Refinements in

LEFT: On October 14, 1947, Captain Charles E. Yeager of the U.S Air Force became the first person to fly faster than the speed of sound, a feat he accomplished in the Glamorous Glennis, a Bell X-1, over Muroc Air Force Base in the California desert.

propeller design that increased the efficiency of the propeller—every hundredth of a percent was considered a major achievement—until a consensus grew among most professionals that the maximum speed any propeller-driven aircraft was going to achieve was 80 percent of the speed of sound. If aircraft were ever going to fly faster (or fly faster than even the speed of sound, and there were some serious doubts about whether that was possible), another type of propulsion was going to be necessary.

Two other kinds were known in the first half of the twentieth century: rocket propulsion and jet propulsion. Rockets were notoriously inefficient fuel guzzlers and were considered highly volatile and uncontrollable. Little hope was held for the use of rockets in aviation for anything but providing short spurts of thrust on takeoffs or in military maneuvers. Jets, on the other hand, though posing problems of their own, were seen by the experts as the most likely power plant type to provide the thrust necessary for high-speed flight. Development of this type of engine was thus followed carefully by aeronautical engineers through the 1930s and 1940s.

THE JET ENGINE

Two historical facts have misled aviation enthusiasts into believing that there was little interest in jet propulsion in the professional aeronautical community before or even during World War II. The first was the fact that Frank Whittle's original 1930 patent for the jet engine was allowed to lapse, and the Whittle plan had to be revived and resurrected in 1936, rescued from the trash heap, as it were. The second was the failure of Ernst Heinkel to convince the Luftwaffe to develop the designs of his engineer Hans von Ohain for a jet-powered fighter aircraft. In both instances, the reasons for the failure had more to do with politics than technical interest. Heinkel's interests were consistently sabotaged by his chief rival, Willy Messerschmitt, throughout the war.

As for Whittle, the early work he had done was submitted as part of a senior thesis at the RAF College at Cramwell. The technicians at the RAF studied Whittle's proposal carefully and recognized that, although he had advanced several novel ideas, most of his work had already been discovered by researchers like Sanford Moss and A.A. Griffith. Had it not been for two classmates of Whittle's who raised the money for further research and Whittle's independent perfection of the jet engine, his ideas probably would not have been developed in England and the jet engine would probably have been developed chiefly in Germany at the end of the war.

It also comes as a great surprise to many aviation enthusiasts how old the idea of jet propulsion really is. In fact, Leonardo da Vinci described a device in his notebooks, which was later widely used in many kitchens, that came to be known as a chimney jack. It involved using the heat from a fire to turn fans in a chimney, which in turn rotated a roasting spit. During the next few centuries, engineers used the concepts of rockets and jet propulsion virtually interchangeably, mainly because in both a rocket and a jet, propulsion is provided by the reaction principle embodied in Newton's third law: to every action there is an equal and opposite reaction. But whereas rockets are self-contained machines that simply spew out propellant in one direction, causing the device to accelerate in the opposite direction, a jet engine is a bit more subtle. A jet engine takes in incoming air just as a propeller does, but instead of merely accelerating the air in the aft direction, thereby propelling the craft forward, the jet engine compresses the air, mixes it with a fuel, combusts (or explodes) it, and sends it spewing out the rear of the engine, where the reaction principle takes over.

OPPOSITE, TOP: A Gloster/ Whittle E. 28/39 experimental aircraft sits in a field awaiting test flight. OPPOSITE, BOTTOM: A British factory produces the first of the Meteors to be deployed in sizable numbers in January 1946. BELOW: By 1951, Gloster Meteors were used extensively by the RAF for European reconnaissance. Shown here is a Gloster Meteor trainer aircraft.

PAGES 48–49: Turbojet engines increased their thrust output prodigiously in the years following World War II, to the point that thrust-to-weight ratios became less important in design. The Pratt & Whitney TF33-P-7 engines shown are each able to deliver 21,000 pounds (9534kg) of thrust and weigh little more than their ancestor, the TF33-P3, used to power the B-52 bomber in the postwar period. ABOVE AND RIGHT: A comparison of the centrifugal-flow engine versus the axial flow. The GE Type I-A (above), based on Whittle's design, has air flow in through intake vanes A and compressed by turbines B and directed into the compressor assembly C and D. The compressed air is then taken by tubes E to the ten combustion chambers F situated around the core of the engine. The exhaust gas spewing out of L also turns the turbines J and K which is connected by shaft N to the front of the engine. This design requires a bulkier engine to accommodate the centrifugal compression. Axial jet engines like the Lycoming XT-58 (right) are sleeker and longer because the compression of the incoming air takes place along the axis of the engine. Aircraft can more easily accommodate longer engines than bulkier ones.

The F100-PW-229 that powers the F-16 is tested at the test facility at Pratt & Whitney, both for the thrust (measured on the "bench") and for efficiency (measured in the tunnel).

Looked at in this way, one can see that there is a significant relationship between the propeller, or prop, engine and the jet engine—both create propulsion by accelerating incoming air rearward. This connection was realized very early on. Although very little experimentation on the application of rockets to aircraft was conducted in the early part of the twentieth century, because it was clear that rockets consumed vast quantities of fuel in very short periods of time, the question of the application of the gas turbine to create jet propulsion was periodically investigated in many quarters almost from the beginning of the history of twentieth-century flight.

As early as 1908, French engineer René Lorin proposed that a piston engine be used not to turn a crankshaft, which in turn would turn a propeller, but to compress incoming air, which would then be ignited, creating a pulse of hot gas that would be expelled from the engine and provide propulsion directly. Lorin encountered the same sort of problem that developers of jet engines would encounter for the next thirty years. The heat tolerances of the metal parts of such an engine lay far beyond the range of metals then known. Almost nothing was known about the kinds of fuel that such machines would require, and the difficulty in controlling the engine made the idea of jet propulsion seem impractical.

In the 1930s, some of the most important work in the development of jet-powered flight took place in Italy. Italy had sponsored a 1935 conference in Rome, the fifth of the so-called Volta Conferences, at which leading aerodynamicists from around the world gathered to discuss the problems and prospects of transonic (near and just exceeding the speed of sound) and supersonic flight. Many of the problems of supersonic flight were worked out at this conference, and though the Italian government attempted to control information that came out of the meeting, the fact that the participants were preeminent researchers from all over the world made such containment difficult. By the late 1930s, therefore, it was clear in most quarters that if a more powerful propulsion system could be developed to replace the propeller, aircraft could and would fly faster than the speed of sound.

Italy, while unable to control the information from the 1935 Volta Conference, certainly had the advantage

of first access to the information, so it is perhaps surprising that the Italian results were so unsuccessful. The Caproni-Campini CC-2 was flown by Mario de Bernardi on August 28, 1940, and was a dismal failure. Not a pure-jet aircraft, it had a radial piston engine driving a compressor system, and attained a top speed of only 205 mph (330kph). Caproni continued to develop the concept, proposing both fighters and bombers, but without success.

Meanwhile, the British involvement in jet engine development had been no more promising. Repeated attempts by Whittle in the early 1930s to interest the British Air Ministry in development of the jet engine were unsuccessful, mainly because Whittle had not solved some of the problems inherent in his design. Whittle used a turbine to compress the incoming air, but the rotors of the turbine of his machine pushed the air outward to the outer wall of the engine, and then the compressed air was allowed to flow to the combustion chamber. The evaluators at the Air Ministry certainly appreciated the problems and passed on the opportunity to invest in solving them. Whittle may well have considered abandoning the project, in spite of the plucky determination he describes himself as having in his autobiography, had two of his Cambridge classmates not approached him and offered assistance in raising the money necessary to create Power Jet Ltd. The company was formed in March 1936 and set out to create a bench model of Whittle's jet engine.

The record books state that the first successful bench test of a jet engine occurred on April 12, 1937, in the laboratories of Power Jet under the supervision of Frank Whittle. Those books go on to credit Frank Whittle (later *Sir* Frank) with the invention of the jet engine and present the British adherence to the centrifugal design as an example of the perseverance of the individual against the blindness of the bureaucracy. Britain's eventual development of the VTOL (Vertical Take Off and Landing) technology behind the Harrier jet fighter is offered as vindication of Whittle's concept.

Quite independently, and without any knowledge of Whittle's work, a young, recently graduated engineer, Dr. Hans von Ohain, secured the interest of Ernst Heinkel in the jet engine. Working with Max Hahn, Ohain created a prototype jet engine that operated on hydrogen, and gave sufficient promise that Heinkel backed the construction of an experimental engine that

LEFT: British perseverance eventually gave them expertise in the technology required for jet-powered Vertical Take Off and Landing (VTOL) aircraft, like the Harrier. Note the unusually large intake ports beneath the cockpit, made necessary by the large mass flow of its high bypass engine. ABOVE: Efficiency is a small price to pay, however, for the adaptability and maneuverability of the aircraft, which is still in use today, shown providing close air support for the USS Nassau in 1989. (This version, the AV-8B, was built under license by McDonnell Douglas for the U.S. Marine Corps.)

also proved to be successful. Heinkel, who was also experimenting with rocket power, had the Heinkel He 178 airframe designed for a von Ohain engine. The combination made the world's first successful jet aircraft flight on August 27, 1939. It was flown by Flight Captain Erich Warsitz, who would also fly the rocket powered He 176.

Fortunately for the Allies, the Nazi government did not give the development of the jet engine the priority that it deserved. Von Ohain knew, as Whittle did, that there had to be advances in metallurgy to withstand the high temperatures generated within jet engines. Both

men also knew that while the jet engine was less complex than a piston engine, it was in its earliest stage of development, and would require time to mature to become an operational engine. As primitive as these early engines were, however, they came at a crucial time, and signaled the dawn of a new era in aviation.

Oddly enough, the engine used on the HE178 was not the axial engine that von Ohain and Hahn had been developing, but a variation of the Whittle engine. In one of the ironies of World War II aviation, Heinkel believed that an adaptation of the Whittle design had a better chance of winning over the German high

During their advance into Germany in January 1945, Allied troops came upon an abandoned Messerschmitt Me 262 in perfect condition, complete with fuel and armament.

command than the novel approach of his two young engineers. By the time the superiority of the axial approach was recognized, the project of implementing jet propulsion on fighter aircraft was taken over by Messerschmitt. The development of a German jet fighter, the Me 262, did not take place until the later stages of the war, and though more than sixteen hundred of them were built and they were superior to the fighters the Allies had produced (whether prop-driven or jet-propelled), the Allied air superiority and the deteriorating ground war rendered the Me 262 too late to influence the outcome of the war.

Many of the leading aerodynamic researchers of Germany found their way to the United States after the war (German rocket scientists, captured by Americans at the end of the war, were not the only important German asset sought after by both American and Russian forces at war's end), including the technical staff that had developed the Heinkel engines. America, though late in entering the jet propulsion field, recognized early on the wisdom of the German approach. After a brief flirtation with Whittle's design, American researchers concentrated on axial designs and turned over the development of jet engines to companies experienced in motor and turbine construction. Thus, the first jet engine built in the United States was the General Electric I-A, a centrifugal design. This engine was placed on an aircraft designed by the Bell Aircraft Co. and resulted in the Bell XP-59A, the first American jet aircraft; its first successful flight took place in October 1942. By the end of the war, GE, Westinghouse, Allison, Curtiss-Wright, and Pratt & Whitney were all developing jet engines, nearly all of which were axial designs.

Suddenly the kind of thrust one would need to attain speeds above the speed of sound—at least 6,000 pounds (2,724kg)—became available. The question remained, however: was it possible to fly faster than the speed of sound? As frequently occurred in the history of aviation, while the answer was never in doubt in the minds of the theoreticians, actually achieving what was theoretically possible would prove a bit more challenging.

LEFT: The Caproni-Campini was an early entry into the jet age by Italy, but proved to be disappointing. It still exists, in the Caproni Museum. BELOW: The Bell P-59 was almost equally disappointing to the United States, although its performance was much superior to the Caproni-Campini. It fell far short of its German counterpart, the Messerschmitt Me 262, and its performance did not exceed contemporary piston engine fighters. PAGES 56–57: The German Messerschmitt Me 262 is conceded to be the finest fighter plane of World War II. Fortunately, poor decisions on the part of the German government delayed its entry into combat until 1944, when it was far too late. If Germany had given the jet engine priority, it is possible that the Me 262 could have been in service in squadron strength in 1943, and very possibly might have delayed the invasion of Europe.

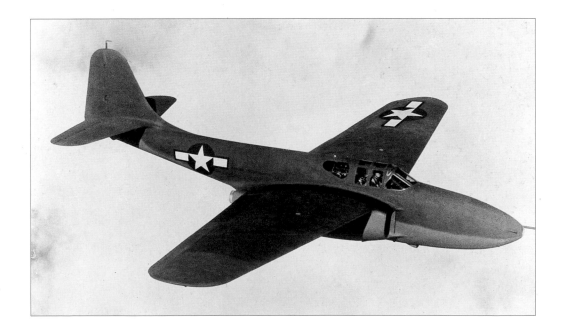

THE SOUND BARRIER

The term "sound barrier" is one used in the popular press. It implied that the speed of sound (about 760 mph at sea level on a standard day) was the upper limit at which an aircraft could fly.

It was well known, of course, that bullets flew faster than sound, but there was concern that the structure of an aircraft would not be able to sustain the stress encountered at supersonic speeds. This concern stemmed in no little degree from the fact that several aircraft, including the Lockheed P-38 and Republic P-47, had encountered severe turbulence when diving at high speeds. Most aeronautical engineers assumed that with proper design of the wings and control surfaces, an aircraft could be flown safely at supersonic speeds. Lockheed conducted many experiments with the P-38 and eventually designed a dive-brake that avoided, rather than solved, the problem.

The question was not whether anything could move faster than sound, but whether anything could *fly* faster than sound. Recall that flight is the result of the aerodynamic forces that act on an airfoil (a wing) as it passes through air. At low speeds, the greater curvature of the upper surface of the wing over the wing's undersurface (its camber) creates a pressure difference between the upper and lower surfaces that results in a net force upward, which is called lift. In the classic presentation of the elementary principles of flight, the source of this pressure difference is the greater speed of the air molecules that pass over the lengthier upper surface of the wing, and as Daniel Bernoulli discovered in the eighteenth century, gas that moves faster exerts less pressure in directions perpendicular to the direction of the flow.

Nearly every schoolchild has seen the following classroom demonstration: hold a sheet of paper at one end in front of your chin and allow the other end to droop out in front of you. When you blow across the top of the curve of the sheet, the drooping end rises because the stationary air under the sheet exerts greater pressure on the paper than the air moving across the top. At low speeds, this is the essence of flight physics; at higher speeds, however—say, above 200 mph (321.8kph) and certainly above 300 mph (482.7kph)—this oversimplification breaks down and the real properties of the atmosphere begin to make themselves felt. The drag that retards the progress of the aircraft is not simply the resistance of the air to the object passing through it (the force of the ambient air on the aircraft, which is called profile drag), but a complex of forces that are determined by the flow of air over the surfaces of the aircraft. Aerodynamicists have many ways of defining and characterizing these sources and varieties of drag, but generally they come in three varieties: induced drag, form drag, and wave drag.

BELOW AND OPPOSITE: The Bell XS-1 (later X-1) exceeded the speed of sound on October 14, 1947. The aircraft was a very pragmatic design, using a bullet-shaped fuselage and thin, straight wings to achieve its design goals. Because fuel was limited, it was designed to do its research flights after being dropped from a B-29 mother-plane. It was capable of taking off from a runway, but the power required to do so cut down on its flight endurance.

Induced drag, a collection of aerodynamic phenomena described by a single name, refers to the resistance to the aircraft created by the lift the airflow creates. This seems paradoxical until we remember that the force that lifts an aircraft is exerted perpendicular to the wing. If the wing is tilted upward, then a component of that force will be acting in a direction opposite to the direction of flight. For high-speed aircraft, which depend more on the lift created by an upward tilt of the thin symmetrical wings (or, in aerodynamic terms, a positive angle of attack) than on the lift created by the camber of the wings, this kind of drag becomes significant.

A kind of induced drag that again becomes a factor in high-speed flight is that caused by the vortices at the end of the wing. Since all wings are finite (no wing goes on and on forever), the air passing over the top of the wing and the air passing underneath meet at the end of the wing, and since there is a difference of pressure (otherwise there would be no lift), the higher-pressure air leaks upward and the lower-pressure air is forced downward. A spiral vortex is created at each wingtip that has a net effect of retarding the flight of the aircraft—in other words, it creates drag. Since the higher pressure of the lower airflow spirals upward around the rear tip, forcing the lower-pressure upper airflow to spiral around the forward edge of the tip, there is a net force pushing the nose of the aircraft downward, as if an unseen hand were pushing the aircraft toward the ground. This phenomenon, known as downwash, was experienced by nearly all the test pilots who flew prop-driven airplanes. It came from a variety of drag sources all related to the type known as induced drag and was a problem for any aircraft that approached 80 percent of the speed of sound.

The second kind of drag (also a collection of aerodynamic phenomena described by a single name), form drag, is also known by a variety of names—parasite drag, skin drag, and interference drag, to name a few. As these names indicate, this type of drag is caused by the physical design of the plane that negates the assumption that air is flowing smoothly over all the surfaces of the aircraft. At high speeds, the small friction between the air and the surface of the aircraft becomes significant, as does the friction between the air and all the places on the aircraft that are not smooth and sleek, or where there is an angle in the design. For example, the angular juncture between the wing and the fuselage is a source of drag, as are the protruding rivets of the body of the fuselage and airfoils.

The same sort of design problems were encountered some years earlier when NACA cowling was placed over the engine and nacelle coverings were placed over the landing gear. These innovations greatly reduced drag during the 1920s, and similar design innovations were possible in the late 1940s, when approaching the speed of sound become attainable.

Every country attempted to design aircraft with a minimum amount of drag, and most prototypes emerged from the shop as very streamlined aircraft. In almost every instance, however, the exigencies of war caused additional equipment to be fitted, which resulted in bumps and irregularities that added drag. A famous examples of this is the Messerschmitt Bf 109, which was saddled with bigger engines, more guns, and more equipment, until the Bf 109G was nicknamed "the Bump" by its pilots because of the many protuberances.

As previously noted, the North American P-51 Mustang came into existence when a British Purchasing Commission came to the United States, seeking to buy additional Curtiss P-40 aircraft. Curtiss was already operating at production capacity, but North American Aviation, in Inglewood, California, was a new firm able to expand its production. North American was invited to build the P-40 under license, a task few companies like to undertake because it not only puts a cap on profits, but it also limits the ability of the company to produce new aircraft of its own design. North American also knew that the P-40 had originated in the Curtiss P-36, a 1935 design. When they approached James H. "Dutch" Kindelberger, president of North American Aviation, he made a counter-offer. North American would design a much better aircraft. The British were naturally interested, but they told him they had to have a prototype of the aircraft in 120 days. From a standing start, then (the story goes), Kindelberger and his designers, Raymond Rice and Edgar Schmued, created the NA-73, the prototype of the Mustang.

The aircraft incorporated the new NASA laminar flow airfoil. While every consideration was given to streamlining the aircraft so that it would have both range and speed, the problems of manufacture were also reviewed. The result was an aircraft that was comparatively easy to manufacture, despite the close tolerances necessary to maintain the laminar flow characteristics of the wing. The aircraft was designed with the standard American liquid cooled engine, the Allison V-1710. In its first

OPPOSITE: The Curtiss P-40 was an excellent aircraft that fought in every theater of the war with success. Even though it often met enemy aircraft of superior performance, its pilots were able to devise tactics that kept the P-40 competitive. Against the Japanese Mitsubishi Zero, for example, the P-40 used dive and zoom tactics and avoided dog-fights. This aircraft is painted in the style of the American Volunteer Group, the famed "Flying Tigers."

ABOVE: James H. "Dutch" Kindelberger, a native West Virginian, was president of North American Aviation in 1940 and developer of the Mustang. His company eventually became the aerospace giant North American Rockwell. OPPOSITE, TOP: The P-51 Mustang was in many minds the greatest prop-driven aircraft ever produced. OPPOSITE, BOTTOM: The Bell P-39N Airacobra, shown here in Tunisia in 1943, had a bulletlike design. PAGES 64–65: One of the mainstays of the Allied air war was the P-51D Mustang.

applications, the P-51 did its best work at low altitudes. The eventual use of the Mustang as an escort for long-range bombers would make it a necessity for the engine to be both high-powered and high-altitude. With suitable modification, the aircraft could accept the Merlin V-1650 engine produced by Rolls-Royce.

The Packard Motor Car Company had been designated to build the Rolls-Royce Merlin engine, and it completed its assignment with great success. Many people have commented that the Packard-built Merlins were in many ways superior to the Rolls-Royce–built versions, particularly in their standardization of parts.

The Mustang became the premier U.S. fighter of the war, replacing both the P-38 and P-47 in the air superiority role. Yet it was not without its faults. When the mature models were fully loaded with fuel, they were marginally stable until the fuel in aft fuselage tank had been burned off.

The Mustang's importance as a fighter in the latter stages of the war derived from the fact that its speed and range made possible the campaign of bombing that was critical to the Allied reconquest of Europe. It would have been a pivotal factor in the bombing and conquest of Japan if the atom bomb hadn't made such a protracted campaign unnecessary. When Hermann Göring first heard about the Mustang, he was incredulous; when he finally became convinced that the Allies really had such an aircraft, he reportedly said, "The war is lost!"

Yet in spite of its importance in winning the air war of World War II, it was what the Mustang was not able to do that drew the attention of the aerodynamic community. It was in the wind tunnel test, and then in the flight tests of the Mustang, that the barriers presented by transonic flight—that is, the regime of flight within 20 percent of the speed of sound—were encountered. These barriers were already well known in lesser planes. A well-publicized crash by test pilot Ralph Virden in 1941 in a P-38 Lightning with design modifications aimed at countering downwash and other drag effects of high-speed flight impressed even the most optimistic theorists with how difficult breaking the sound barrier would be. The Mustang pushed piston engine fighter design to a peak, but there were other fighters from other nations that came close to matching its performance. Fortunately, the Mustang was available in much greater quantity than the others.

BREAKING THE SOUND BARRIER

The Mustang's problems arose from the third kind of drag, and this drag was not going to respond to design improvements for the simple reason that it is caused not by the plane but by the interaction of the air around the plane. Wave drag arises because the air molecules moving faster than the speed of sound collide into their slower neighbors and disrupt the flow altogether, destroying any lift created by a difference in flow-induced air pressure. The colliding air molecules create a shock wave that travels out from the source of the shock—the location of this "damming up" of the air particles—in a cone shape behind the object moving faster than the speed of sound.

This phenomenon of the sonic shock wave had been well known since the late nineteenth century; it was predicted, described, and even photographed as early as 1887 by Austrian physicist Ernst Mach, after whom the unit of speed equal to the speed of sound in any medium is named. (Thus, we speak of a speed of 769 mph [1,237.3kph] at sea level or a speed of 660 mph [1,061.9kph] at an altitude of 40,000 feet [12,192m] as being Mach 1. The term was coined in 1929 by Swiss engineer Jacob Ackert. Though Ernst Mach is known primarily for his experiments in supersonic airflow, he was also the foremost of a very small group of late-nineteenth-century scientists who were dissatisfied with classical physics and paved the way with their criticisms for the revolution of relativity and quantum physics in the first decades of the twentieth century.) Using a technique known as Schlieren photography, in which differences in gas density are made visible and thus

photographable, Mach showed that a projectile flowing through the air faster than the speed of sound would create a shock wave at both ends of the projectile that would trail out from the projectile in a cone. Mach thus correctly predicted what many have observed when a plane passes overhead at supersonic speeds: that the thud of the sonic boom comes in very close pairs. These are the booms created by the two cones that emanate from the aircraft, one cone from the nose and the other from the tail.

It was not until the 1930s that wind tunnels were created that could produce supersonic airflow. One might think that this development would dispel any doubts about the possibility of breaking through the sound barrier. But the effects of airflow at transonic speeds are so chaotic that the bouncing of air off the walls of the wind tunnels introduced a confusing element in the experiments. Oddly enough, the problems disappeared in tests with airflows higher than Mach 1.2. If an aircraft could reach Mach 1 and continue aloft to beyond 1.2, a new set of equations and airflow dynamics would take over and the flight would proceed smoothly. It was only in the transonic range—between 80 and 120 percent of the speed of sound—that uncertainty reigned. As the 1940s dawned, engineers and aerodynamicists felt that the question would not be settled until an aircraft actually flew faster than the speed of sound.

The first official attempt to break the sound barrier was made in 1946 by the British. The de Havilland family has made incredible contributions to the history of aviation as well as great sacrifices to the development of flight. One of the more dramatic (though oddly unheralded in the literature) was made by Geoffrey de Havilland, son and namesake of the patriarch of the de Havillands. In the fall of 1946, the British were eager to press their technology of the jet engine into service and to seize the opportunity to lead aviation into the jet age and supersonic flight. The craft chosen was the DH-108 Swallow, an experimental aircraft that incorporated Frank Halford's de Havilland Goblin engine. The design of the Swallow was remarkably advanced: it had a swept wing and no tail assembly, the cockpit was sleekly built into the fuselage, and the air intake ducts were built into the wings of the plane. The swept wing had first been suggested by German aerodynamicist Adolf Busemann as a means of preventing the shock wave from the nose of a plane from interacting with the aircraft's wings.

After several weeks of flight testing at speeds up to Mach .8, on September 27, 1946, Geoffrey de Havilland attempted to break the sound barrier. As the aircraft passed Mach .9 (at that altitude 556 mph [894.6kph]), it began to experience severe downwash. The large wings of the aircraft gave the pilot greater control, but the aircraft structure could not take the great pressure being placed on the airframe by the shock wave beginning to build up on the plane's surface. Somewhere around 590 mph (949.3kph), the Swallow disintegrated and de Havilland was killed instantly. His death sent a pall through the aviation community; in the United States, the determination to break the sound barrier became even stronger.

In 1944, the Army Air Force and NACA, determined to build an experimental aircraft that would fly faster than sound, awarded a contract to Bell Aircraft Corporation of Buffalo, New York, to build a plane that would fly at 800 mph (1,287.2kph) at 35,000 feet (10,668m). All the elements for this undertaking were in place. The aerodynamicist Theodore von Karman had calculated that the thrust required was 6,000 pounds (2,724kg); this was more than could reliably be supplied by a jet engine, causing the engineers to consider a rocket engine. The test performed at the NACA supersonic wind tunnel at Langley by Ezra Kotcher indicated that a swept wing would not be necessary for supersonic flight. Instead, a conventional straight wing with a thin profile was selected. Bell designed the wing to be very strong; indeed, before the age of computers, aircraft were generally conservatively designed for safety. The short duration of power available from rocket engines made engineers assume from the start that the first aircraft to break the sound barrier would be carried aloft in the bay of a larger aircraft, establish its records, and then glide down to a very long runway.

Bell Aircraft Corporation was a suitable choice for this assignment. Under the direction of its chief engineer, Robert Woods, Bell had created a number of innovative designs during the war, notably the P-39 Airacobra, a plane that was widely used by the Soviet Air Force under the Lend-Lease program, and the Bell XP-59A Airacomet, the first American jet airplane. The Bell engineers decided on a bulletlike design, which was thought to be perfect for the aircraft that would break through the sound barrier. Work began in earnest in December 1944.

ABOVE: The young Chuck Yeager in a photo taken the day of his historic flight. ABOVE, TOP: A Bell X-1A rocket plane. Yeager set another speed record when he piloted a Bell X-1A to a speed of 1,650 mph (2,655kph).

By the end of 1945, the first of three models, which was designated the Bell XS-1 (experimental sonic-1) but later known as the X-1, rolled out of the assembly hangar in Buffalo. The plane was small by the day's standards, just 38 feet (11.5m) long with a wingspan of 28 feet (8.5m). A great deal of discussion surrounded the question of the thickness of the wings—the thinner the wing, the later in the pre-Mach 1 speed range the aircraft would encounter the problems that led to the death of de Havilland. The feeling was that the plane would be powerful and structurally strong enough to push its way through the problem speeds and punch through the sound barrier. This approach was tested successfully in the later versions of the X-1, but the first model had very thin airfoils. The only things missing were the engines; they were still being built by Reaction Motors, Inc. (RMI), a small company in Pompton Plains, New Jersey. RMI had developed a rocket engine that was able to provide a high thrust without the volatility of standard liq-

uid rocket engines. (The secret to the RMI engine was that it burned a less volatile mixture of liquid oxygen and diluted alcohol. Also, the pump controls were more sophisticated so that the pilot could monitor and control the engine more readily.)

The initial gliding test of the X-1, at Pinecastle Field near Orlando, Florida, showed the craft to be airworthy and a nimble flier. Tests of the fully engined X-1 did not take place until December 1946, under the dark cloud created by the death of Geoffrey de Havilland and by Bell test pilot Jack Woolams, who had died in an air racing accident earlier in the year. The test pilot for the early trials was Bell's Chalmers "Slick" Goodlin, but the Army Air Force and NACA had spent so much on the project that they insisted an AAF test pilot be the one to break the sound barrier. Goodlin was replaced by then relatively unknown Charles E. "Chuck" Yeager, a twenty-four-year-old AAF test pilot who had demonstrated his ability and bravery during the war.

By now the test area had been moved to Muroc, an airfield carved out of the 65-square-mile (168.3 sq km) Rogers Dry Lake in a remote area of California's Mojave Desert. Muroc had been a lonely outpost where some test flights of experimental aircraft had taken place. Now it had become a bustling center of aviation engineering; it would eventually become Edwards Air Force Base. The test pilots at Muroc spent their off hours at the Fly Inn, a bar run by former barnstormer Florence "Pancho" Barnes, who earned her nickname flying in guns to Mexican revolutionaries in the 1920s. It was here that the legends grew about the daring test pilots who proved the planes developed by the newly formed U.S. Air Force, and it was from this group that the first astronaut corps (the men with "the right stuff") was eventually recruited.

Yeager began testing the engines on the X-1 (now dubbed *Glamorous Glennis* by Yeager, after his wife) in August 1947, making test flights that brought him clos-

er and closer to Mach 1. During these tests, it became clear that the critical point at which the shock waves created by the aircraft would interfere with the aircraft flying was Mach .94. Once this point was passed, the X-1 would stand a good chance of passing Mach 1.

On October 14, 1947, the historic flight took place. Yeager, who had injured himself in a horse-riding accident the day before but neglected to tell anyone for fear he would be replaced, settled into the snug cockpit of the X-1, his chest aching from what he later discovered were two broken ribs sustained in the accident. The B-29 with the X-1 in its bay took off at 10:02 A.M., and at 10:26, with the B-29 at 20,000 feet (6,096m), ground controller Bob Cardenas made his contribution to aerospace culture by spontaneously counting down from ten to mark the release of the X-1 from its mother aircraft.

At first the X-1 plummeted downward; a few seconds later, when Yeager was certain he was clear of the B-29, he powered two of the four engines and was flying

ABOVE: Florence "Pancho" Barnes was a figure in flight legend and lore for her record-setting flights in the Beech Mystery Ship in the 1930s and for her role in the Muroc supersonic test-pilot culture.

The X-1A, along with the X-1B, laid the foundation for the development of supersonic fighter aircraft.

BELOW: Yeager receives a congratulatory handshake from Lawrence D. Bell, the visionary who had built the X-1 and other X-series aircraft. The photo was staged several months after the record-setting flight, and Yeager has his foot on the ladder of the X-1A. RIGHT: The X-1A, along with the X-1B, laid the foundation for the development of supersonic fighter aircraft.

behind 6,000 pounds (2,724kg) of thrust. He climbed to 42,000 feet (12,801.6m) and then lit the third chamber. The X-1 burst forward, and just before the fuel gauge pointed to "empty," the tachometer jumped and a double sonic boom was heard across the desert. Yeager then cut his engines, ejected the last of his fuel, and glided to a soft landing on the lake bed, hearing only the wind passing his cockpit window and the clicking of his instrument panel clock.

The world did not learn of Yeager's feat for eight months because the flight was classified. But that night at the Fly Inn, Pancho Barnes treated Yeager to a steak— and the drinks were on the house.

CHAPTER THREE

THE
QUEST FOR SPEED

ONCE THE SOUND BARRIER HAD BEEN PIERCED, THE RACE WAS ON FOR EVER HIGHER SPEEDS AND THE CREATION OF AIRCRAFT CAPABLE OF SUPERSONIC AND HYPERSONIC FLIGHT.

Hypersonic flight is usually arbitrarily defined as speeds above Mach 5, though nothing unusual happens, aerodynamically speaking, at that speed. The effects and obstacles of supersonic flight are evident as soon as the sound barrier is crossed, and they simply increase in magnitude as speed increases. There are three main problem areas of hypersonic flight: the adverse effects of the shock waves created on the airflow across the wings and body of an aircraft, the problems these shock waves and supersonic airflow in general pose to propulsion systems, and the great increase in temperature at hypersonic speeds due to air friction and the effect these very high temperatures have on aircraft systems and on the survival of the pilots (and passengers, if there are any).

As often happens, the practical applications of cutting-edge research come only after the new territory is charted. In the case of supersonic flight, as the experimental aircraft forged ahead into ever higher speed realms, what was learned in dealing with each of the obstacles was applied, mainly to the creation of advanced fighters. Allowances are made for experimental aircraft that are not viable inside other aircraft that serve a particular purpose: an experimental aircraft has the luxury of taking off from the belly of a B-52 bomber and landing on the dry bed of a salt flat several miles long. An experimental aircraft can carry a single well-conditioned pilot and keep that pilot alive by dedicating a significant portion of the craft to providing a comfortable (or at least inhabitable) area the size of a steamer trunk, and then only with the help of special pressurized-flight-suit technology.

The story of high-speed flight after October 14, 1947, takes place along three distinct historical lines of research, all developing out of the initial research done in the

LEFT: The McDonnell Douglas F-15E Strike Eagle is a remarkable adaptation of the original F-15 air superiority fighter.

development of the Bell X-1 and intersecting with others at certain critical points. One line involves the creation of the X-series of aircraft, culminating in the Bell X-15, the first hypersonic aircraft. These aircraft were designed and flown to expand the boundaries of aviation knowledge. They reached the highest altitudes and speeds every obtained by experimental aircraft, and paved the way for a host of later designs. While considered expensive at the time, these test aircraft were remarkable bargains for the results they achieved. Given their great advance in performance, their safety record was remarkable, a tribute to their pilots and engineers.

The second line of research involves the creation of aircraft capable of high speeds for sustained periods and with maneuverability that is of use in a combat setting. The objective now is tactical, and there are ways in which some capabilities are sacrificed to create advantages in others

that will result in gains in the battlefield. This line begins with the creation of the North American F-86 Sabre, and from there goes to the entire series of fighter aircraft developed by the United States, the Soviet Union, and France, leading eventually to the creation of the Lockheed SR-71 Blackbird, which has come to be used as a spy plane but was originally conceived as a fighter prototype (and which may yet give birth to the next generation of tactical fighter aircraft). Another way of regarding these first two lines of research is that the first dealt with rocket-powered aircraft, the second with jet-powered aircraft.

Finally, the application of all this technology to commercial transportation led to the creation of supersonic transport (SST) aircraft. The United States and the Soviet Union both believed the creation of a viable SST was an important goal on the propaganda front of the Cold War. The United States declined to build an SST, but the

Soviet Union succeeded. In the end, the most successful SST turned out to be the product of a French-British collaboration: the Concorde. Though it operates at a huge loss, it remains in service for prestige purposes. Yet the attempt to create mass supersonic air transport continues, and the drawing boards of the major manufacturers are never bereft of new blueprints of proposed SSTs.

THE X-SERIES

The X-1 in which Chuck Yeager made history on October 14, 1947, was flown for several years and continued to break records. Yeager himself reached Mach 1.35 in the *Glamorous Glennis* less than a month after his record-breaking flight. The X-2, a new design with swept wings, was commissioned in 1945; but development of the plane, which was designed to break Mach 3, took more than five years and it did not fly until October 1952. In the meantime, Douglas produced the X-3, a sleek white airplane with a wingspan of just 23 feet (7m) that immediately earned the nickname "the Flying Stiletto." The X-3, for all its imposing appearance, was not the product of the same sort of exhaustive wind tunnel testing as the X-1 or the developing X-2. But it did have an advanced power plant and served as a useful testing platform for the ramjet engines that would become standard for the hypersonic flight realm. The power plant of the X-1 was a rocket engine, which means that both the fuel and the oxidizer in which the fuel burns

BELOW: The F-100 Super Sabre, first flown in 1953, was the world's first operational supersonic fighter and served with distinction in Vietnam as a fighter-bomber.

(the largely oxygen-laced mixture that takes up most of the room in the fuselage tanks) were contained within the aircraft. If long-duration supersonic flight was ever to become a reality, a way would have to be found to relieve the aircraft of the burden of carrying its own oxygen, and that meant intake ducts that would direct and compress the air in a jet engine configuration.

Not surprisingly, the various standard turbojet configurations did not work in supersonic flight—at least not well. The shock waves created inside the turbine wreaked havoc with the airflow and made it impossible to control. Ramjets, however, do not use turbines; they depend on the simple compression of the incoming airflow as a result of the funnel shape of the intake duct. Wind tunnel tests further showed that the right geometry for the air intake could direct the shock waves to assist in the compression of the air and actually improve the engine's performance. Although structural and control problems kept the X-3 from ever attaining Mach 2, the speed for which it was designed, a great deal was learned about ramjet design and the problems that future supersonic aircraft would have to overcome.

Mach 2 was achieved by the fighters that the U.S. Air Force had developed during the Korean War and in the early stages of the Cold War by the time the X-2 was ready. The aircraft was considered highly unstable by

engineer and test pilot alike, though test pilot Pete Everest had, on July 23, 1956, achieved a new world speed record of Mach 2.87 in the X-2. The attempt to break Mach 3 in the X-2 was assigned to Korean War fighter ace and test pilot Captain Iven Kincheloe. (If the name sounds familiar, you may recall that a character in the situation comedy *Hogan's Heroes*—which was about downed Allied pilots in a German prisoner-of-war camp, or *luftstalag*—was named Iven Kincheloe. The show's creators chose the name in honor of the real Captain Kincheloe, who was killed in 1958 during a routine flight in an F-104 just after being named as the test pilot of the landmark X-15.)

On September 10, 1956, Kincheloe took the X-2 to 126,200 feet (38,465.7m) and cut the engines, intending to nose the plane downward and break Mach 3 in the dive back to earth. But the aircraft began to roll and Kincheloe concentrated on regaining control of it. By the time he reached the top of his upward coast, he had set an unofficial altitude record of 161,000 feet (49,072.8m). Kincheloe had 90 percent of the earth's atmosphere under him; he could plainly make out the curvature of the earth, and the sun was a bright white spot in the black sky above him. He was not able to break Mach 3 on his dive, but the feat earned him the nickname "the first man in space."

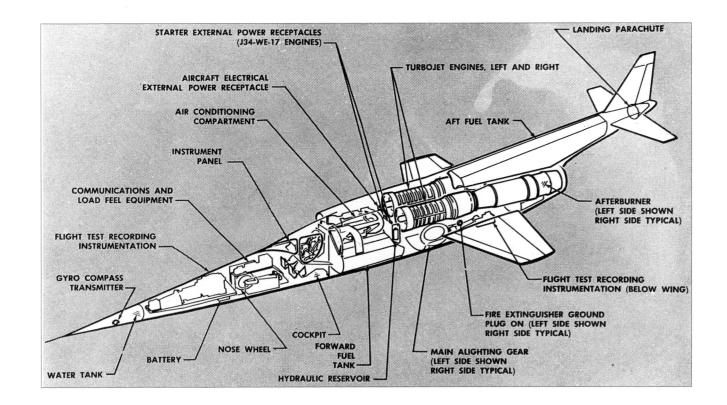

OPPOSITE AND LEFT: The lessons learned in developing the X-3 proved valuable to Douglas in later fighter design. Unlike the X-1 planes, the X-3 was not a large fuel tank on which rode a pilot. The aircraft had supersonic capabilities and room for sophisticated electronics.

ABOVE: Clarence "Kelly" Johnson was the legendary leader of the Lockheed "Skunk Works," where some of the most innovative aircraft ever created were designed and built. BELOW: One of Johnson's early successes was the P-80 (later called the F-80) "Shooting Star," a jet-powered fighter, shown here in a test using ramjet engines on its wingtips to improve performance. This "naive" pragmatism allowed Johnson to dare to try ideas others dismissed out of hand.

A final attempt to break Mach 3 in the X-2 was made on September 27. The pilot, Captain Milburn "Mel" Apt, was inexperienced in the X-2, though he was a veteran of the F-100 and had flown over Mach 2 many times. His work in the X-2 flight simulator had gone smoothly. Kincheloe would be flying the chaser aircraft and would be in constant radio contact with Apt throughout the flight. As Apt climbed to 70,000 feet (21,336m) everything was looking good. He indicated that he was cutting his engines and going into his dive. But as the plane nosed down, Apt lost control and the aircraft began turning end over end. Apt was knocked unconscious for a few seconds. When he came to, he realized the plane was going to crash. He pressed the ejection button, and the entire nose, which was designed as an escape capsule, jettisoned. Before Apt could eject from the capsule, he was again knocked unconscious; the capsule plummeted to the ground and Apt was killed instantly in the crash.

The death of Mel Apt ended the X-2 project, but not the desire to break Mach 3 and beyond. It was at this point that two lines of aeronautics diverged: while North American Aviation was given the contract to develop the X-15 rocket plane (largely as a testing platform for the burgeoning U.S. space program), Lockheed was contracted to develop a jet-powered aircraft that would

achieve speeds in excess of Mach 5. Both planes were completed largely through the determined efforts of the chief engineers for the projects, Clarence "Kelly" Johnson at Lockheed and Harrison Storms, North American's largely (until quite recently) unsung chief engineer.

Work on the X-15 began in earnest in 1955, and the order was a tall one: the X-15 was supposed to be able to achieve Mach 7 and an altitude of 264,000 feet (80,467.2m). There were many problems to be solved, to be sure. A whole new regime of wind tunnel tests would have to be conducted to solve the stability problems that had plagued the X-2 and the X-3. The engines being used were of the same basic design as those used on the X-1. Those engines provided a maximum of 8,000 pounds (3,632kg) of thrust; the X-15 would, it was calculated, require engines seven times as powerful. Such engines were still on the drawing board and had not even been bench-tested in 1955. And at speeds above Mach 3, the thermal properties of the aircraft's skin were going to become critical. Although the calculated (and tested) temperature of the skin of an aircraft at Mach 7 was over 4,000°F (2,204°C), which is higher than the melting point of stainless steel, no alloy then in production or even contemplated could withstand temperatures higher than 2,000°F (1,093°C).

In what has finally been recognized as a heroic effort by Storms and his team, North American rolled out the first X-15 on October 15, 1958. Every problem had been tackled and solved. The aircraft was given a great measure of control by the addition of twin rudders on top of and on the underside of the aircraft. Though the first models of the X-15 still relied on the old Reaction Motors LR11 rocket engines, the aircraft was soon outfitted with the new RMI XLR99 engines, capable of providing 57,000 pounds (25,878kg) of thrust. The thermal problems were solved by the judicious use of titanium alloys and a coolant system that would allow the aircraft to fly at Mach 6 and above without burning up. The arrival of the X-15 was timely because the Soviets had orbited Sputnik I just a year earlier, a feat that had damaged the reputation of America's space program.

The X-15, piloted by Scott Crossfield, established the first of a string of records that would be broken by the aircraft when, on August 4, 1960, it flew at Mach 3.31; eight days later, it established a new official altitude record of 136,500 feet (41,605.2m). On June 27, 1962, the X-15, piloted by Joe Walker, finally achieved hypersonic flight with a speed of 4,159 mph (6,691.8kph). The following year, Walker took the X-15 to an altitude of an astounding 354,200 feet, or 67.08 miles (107,960.1m or 107.9km). In a program that consisted of 199 test flights (the aircraft stubbornly resisted attempts at a ceremonial two hundredth flight), every element of the X-15 was tested and redesigned; clearly the intention even then was to produce systems that would later be used in hypersonic aircraft.

The X-15's crowning achievement was the speed record of 4,534 mph (7,295.2kph)—Mach 6.72—achieved with Major Pete Knight piloting on October 3, 1967. Both records—Knight's speed and Walker's altitude—still stand today. (Even then they were broken by spacecraft, not aircraft. In fact, the highest speed ever attained by a human being was Mach 36—or 24,290 mph (39,082.6kph)—achieved by several astronauts during reentry of the Apollo space modules.)

ABOVE: This mock cockpit of the X-15 is deceptively simple—except for the ejection apparatus at left, the controls do not look all that different from conventional avionics of the time. The display was changed, however, for this publicity shot to keep the method used by the pilot to monitor and control the fuel, and thus the range and abilities of the plane, secret. PAGE 80: X-15 test pilot Neil Armstrong (later to gain fame as the first man to walk on the Moon) points to the "Q-Ball" on the nose of the aircraft—the sensor that adjusts the aircraft's attitude to minimize heating from air friction at hypersonic speeds. PAGE 81, TOP AND BOTTOM: Unlike the earlier X-aircraft, the X-15 was too long to launch from the bomb bay of the B-59, so it was carried aloft under the wing of a B-52 bomber.

It should be noted that the X-15, like the X-1, was carried aloft and launched from a B-52 jet bomber. Thus, by some standards, these records are tainted (or at least asterisked) by the fact that the aircraft did not take off from a standing start on earth. Such record flights would be made in due course, but there is no doubt that the X-15 flew (and that it was not rocketed into space and then left to glide back, as is the case with the Space Shuttle orbiter) and that a number of configurations for additional jet engines (which would have been jettisoned once aloft) were available to the X-series of aircraft, which would have enabled them to qualify...unasterisked.

THE FIGHTERS AND BOMBERS

The application of high-speed aviation obviously was of great interest to the air forces of the world, beginning in World War II and continuing into the Cold War. But this aspect of the quest for speed was soon found to have its limits: military air strategists relearned a lesson first demonstrated by the British in the Battle of Britain, namely that coordinated tactics guided by superior field knowledge could allow inferior aircraft to overcome an enemy's air power that was superior in performance and number. In the modern era, the advent of more modern

radar equipment and the deployment of airborne radar and communication centers in the form of AWACS (Airborne Warning and Control Systems)—aircraft which are, in effect, Boeing 707s with radar dishes mounted on top of the fuselages—allowed air forces with second-line fighters and bombers to nullify the air superiority of an enemy. (The American response has been to develop stealth aircraft that render AWACS useless, again shifting the balance toward the side that has superior field reconnaissance and not necessarily superior aircraft.)

This was how the British were able to thwart the Nazi attempt to gain control of the skies of Great Britain in World War II, even though the Luftwaffe's planes were, for a time, superior to the aircraft the RAF was putting in the air. It was also a factor in the standoff between the American air forces in Korea and the North Korean air forces, which consisted of Soviet-supplied MiG-15s flown by both Chinese and Russian pilots. The MiGs were shot down by the American F-86 Sabres by a ratio of fourteen to one, but the U.S.-led forces were not able to establish a clear control of the airspace over Korea because the North Koreans confined the engagements to areas they controlled and in which they had strong radar installations. This was what defined the so-called MiG Alley, in which nearly all of the air engagements took place. (MiG Alley was also defined by the Communist forces as those areas where they could be certain of rescuing downed pilots. This was important to the ongoing

Soviet policy of denying that Russian pilots were flying the MiGs, a claim that would have been exposed if many Russian pilots had been captured in downed fighters. This is why the high kill ratio of Sabres to MiGs is misleading. Based on the performance of the planes and the capabilities of Soviet pilots, if Russian pilots had been allowed to engage American air forces conventionally in the skies over Korea and had not been ordered to avoid being downed and captured, resulting in the fact that most downed MiG pilots were Chinese and, to a lesser extent, North Korean, many experts believe the ratio would have been more even for the simple reason that the MiG-15 was every bit as good a performer as the F-86, especially at high altitudes, where most of the skirmishing took place.)

Both the F-86 Sabre and the MiG-15 have their development roots in the Volta Conference of 1935 (see chapter 2). While the Italians were impressing the aerodynamics community with a tour of facilities where a Mach 2.7 wind tunnel was under construction (and Mussolini was casting a pall over the conference by using it to announce Italy's invasion of Ethiopia), an unknown German engineer named Adolf Busemann, then only thirty-four years old, presented a paper in which he suggested that a supersonic aircraft would perform better if its wings were "swept back" at an angle from the fuselage. This would allow the shock wave that was formed at the nose of the plane and that radiated out in a cone to miss the aircraft's wings altogether.

ABOVE: The Boeing B-47 Stratojet, an innovative bomber design, was the foundation of the United States Strategic Air Command (SAC) during the 1950s. OPPOSITE: An Air Force publicity shot demonstrates the size of the B-52 bomb bay.

Now, anyone who has made a paper airplane may wonder why this idea was so novel in 1935 and why it was greeted with mild derision by the other attendees. Doesn't it seem obvious that an aircraft with swept-back wings would pierce through the air more efficiently and offer less resistance to the oncoming air and thus less drag to impede the flight of the aircraft? One must remember, however, that Busemann was not concerned with reducing drag; he was concerned with eliminating the disruptive effects of the shock wave created by super-sonic flight. In fact, the problem of reducing drag (that is, the profile drag of the wing) was addressed universal-ly by aerodynamicists by making the wing thinner. Sweeping back the wing cut down drastically on the lift it provided since only that component of the airflow per-pendicular to the front edge of the wing provided lift. Busemann calculated that, for most purposes, this was a small price to pay at supersonic speeds for avoiding the interference of the shock wave with the wing's per-formance. Thus, most of the early jet aircraft, like the Messerschmitt ME262 and the British Gloster Meteor, and indeed the first supersonic aircraft, like the Bell X-1, all had conventional wings. (The ME262 had very slightly swept wings designed to improve the aircraft's center of gravity, which incidentally improved its super-sonic performance.

Since supersonic flight was considered a long way off, most of those attending the 1935 Volta Conference ignored Busemann's findings, though careful notes were taken and preserved by many (because one never knows). At the end of the war, both American and Russian scientists accompanied the liberating armies in scooping up German scientists and recruiting them to their respective sides in the already developing Cold War. One of those scientists in the American camp (in the enterprise that was known as Operation Paperclip) was aerodynamicist Theodore von Karman, a Hungarian-born scientist who had immigrated to the United States in 1936. Von Karman worked at the California Institute of Technology and consulted with the preeminent air-craft manufacturers of the day. When he came across Busemann in a forgotten laboratory near Brunswick, Austria, the young scientist reminded von Karman of their meeting in Rome and of Busemann's paper on the swept wing. Von Karman described it as akin to being struck by lightning when he realized the value of Busemann's work and of work then being done inde-pendently back in the United States by researcher

Robert T. Jones, a self-taught aerodynamics engineer working at NACA's Langley Laboratory who had been in touch with von Karman. It was then that von Karman initiated a special effort to capture aerodynamics engi-neers (until then the focus was on rockets and atomic power), and as a result many important aerodynamicists, including Voigt, immigrated to America.

The effect of Busemann's work was immediate. Many plans to create straight-wing aircraft were scrapped, and engineers went back to the drawing board to incorporate the wind tunnel data into their designs (it was noted that along with these scientists came—to both their American and Soviet hosts—many volumes of laboratory data). A straight-wing jet bomber being designed by Boeing was redrawn to accommo-date the swept wing, resulting in the B-47 bomber, forerunner of the great Boeing bombers produced over the next four decades. The B-47 had a top speed of 600 mph (965.4kph) and was known to test pilots as the "six-engine fighter." Similarly, the design team led by Raymond Rice at North American raced with the Russians to produce a swept-wing fighter and won the race by a scant thirteen weeks. The North American F-86 Sabre became the first operational aircraft designed for combat to break the sound barrier, on April 26, 1948, piloted by celebrated World War II ace and test pilot George Welch.

Meanwhile, Busemann's findings were being applied by Artem Mikoyan and Mikhail Gurevich (founders of MiG) in creating the MiG-15, a plane that had many advantages over the F-86, though not in terms of raw level-flight speed; by Marcel Dassault in France in creat-ing the Mystère in 1951; and by Britain's Sidney Camm, who produced the Hawker Hunter in 1953.

To be sure, not every designer availed himself of Busemann's solution. Lockheed's Kelly Johnson, who had designed the P-80 Shooting Star, America's first jet fighter and a subsonic (Mach .8) aircraft, used the same straight-wing configuration that appeared on the X-series aircraft in developing the famed F-104 Starfighter, the first Mach 2 jet fighter (and the plane about which a test pilot quipped, "It looks like it's doing Mach 2 just sitting in the hangar"), which relied on the short length of the wing to keep its surface inside the shock wave cone at supersonic speeds. Thus, within the community of designers, there were two approaches: one using short, straight wings, and the other using swept wings. The advantage of the swept wing was that it allowed for

bulkier fuselages, which meant they could accommodate bigger armament and more bombs.

With very few exceptions, the swept wing aircraft was used on almost all supersonic fighters. This design fact, coupled with the great increase in engine power, led to the introduction of supersonic fighters in all the major air forces of the world. The Lockheed F-104 Starfighter, produced by Kelly Johnson's Skunk Works, was one of the few supersonic fighters not to use swept wings. Its wings were both short and very thin, and while used in great numbers by foreign air forces, the F-104 was not used extensively by the USAF. Swept wing fighters were not devoid of problems however, and benefited from the development of computers-aided flight controls that could anticipate and dampen their undesirable characteristics.

The breakthrough in supersonic aircraft design came in the laboratory in December 1951, when Richard T. Whitcomb, an aerodynamicist at NACA's Langley facility, discovered that he could eliminate this drag by pinching the body of the fuselage in such a way that the total cross section of the aircraft remained constant for the length of the wing. As the cross section increases because there is more wing, the fuselage shrinks. This was dubbed the area rule and was applied to the Convair F-102 delta-winged fighter aircraft, a highly powered machine that refused to break through Mach 1. With the redesigned fuselage,-pinched in so that it resembled a soda bottle, giving rise to the term "Coke bottle design," the aircraft's speed with the same propulsion system was boosted an incredible 20 percent, making it one of the more effective early supersonic fighters.

The F-86 Sabre evolved very naturally into the F-100 Super Sabre, though the transition was anything but routine. The Super Sabre was originally designated the Sabre 45 because the sweep had gone from 35 to 45 degrees. The plane was designed to be the first jet fighter that could cruise and fight at supersonic speeds. The Super Sabre was in the grand tradition of aircraft that represent so great an advance over their predecessors that it seems impossible that they come so close on their predecessors' heels. The aircraft was long and sleek, the Coke bottle pinch in its fuselage barely noticeable. The bubble canopy was built into the plane's smooth lines and the wings were only half as thin as the F-86's, with a wingspan of only 37 feet (11.2m).

LEFT: After bearing most of the brunt for the early air combat in the skies over Korea, the F-80 Shooting Star saw service as a reconnaissance aircraft, particularly as a drone (pilotless, remote-control) aircraft. BELOW: By the time the United States had developed the F-100 Super Sabre, a jet fighter far superior to the MiG-15, the Korean War was over and the Russians had also gone on to develop a new generation of fighters.

The early tests of the aircraft conducted in May 1953 revealed a design flaw that made the aircraft difficult to control at low and at very high speeds. Many of the problems had been noted in the test flights of the F-86, but those problems could be corrected by minor adjustments to the rudder or the engines. Such Band-Aid solutions were not available to the F-100, and the final report by the principal test pilot for the program, Pete Everest, recommended against deployment of the aircraft until these problems were solved. Test pilots are, by nature, a cautious lot, so this development should have, at the very least, prompted an evaluation of the program at the highest levels. Instead the air force, responding to the pressures of the Cold War, forged ahead and, by the end of 1954, had deployed seventy Super Sabres. Although the F-100 was the first fighter able to cruise and fight at supersonic speeds, the problems about

which Everest had warned severely limited the plane's usefulness in the field. The only saving grace was that the aircraft's Soviet counterpart, the MiG-19, had the same stability problems. Such were the pressures of the arms race that both superpowers deployed aircraft with certain highly publicized capabilities but that were of limited usefulness in combat situations. By the time the problems of the F-100 Super Sabre were solved, with those solutions (increasing the wingspan, raising the tailfin, and installing a more sophisticated flap assembly) lowering its speed in landing, the Super Sabre found its main use as the aircraft of the aerobatics team of the U.S. Air Force, the Thunderbirds.

During the decade after 1954, when the United States was sorting out its problems with the Super Sabre and doing the enormous amount of research necessary for the development of the F-111, the U-2, and the

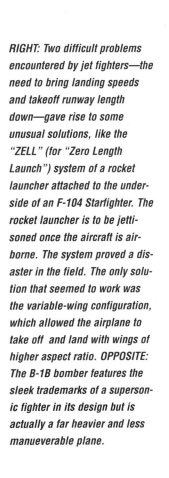

RIGHT: Two difficult problems encountered by jet fighters—the need to bring landing speeds and takeoff runway length down—gave rise to some unusual solutions, like the "ZELL" (for "Zero Length Launch") system of a rocket launcher attached to the underside of an F-104 Starfighter. The rocket launcher is to be jettisoned once the aircraft is airborne. The system proved a disaster in the field. The only solution that seemed to work was the variable-wing configuration, which allowed the airplane to take off and land with wings of higher aspect ratio. OPPOSITE: The B-1B bomber features the sleek trademarks of a supersonic fighter in its design but is actually a far heavier and less manueverable plane.

SR-71 (and the same sort of scrambling seems to have been going on behind the Iron Curtain, since the bureaucratic snafu plays no favorites to political systems or ideologies), the European countries had the opportunity to catch up and in some areas surpass the superpowers. Sweden deployed the Saab 35 Draken in 1955—a Mach 1.5 fighter that was briefly the most advanced fighter in the world—and the Viggen in 1967. France's Dassault (now merged with Breguet) built a series of great fighters, including the Mystère series and the Mirage III, Mirage V, and Mirage 2000, each a supersonic fighter that was, when introduced, at the cutting edge of performance.

Time and resources were on the side of the superpowers, though, and the American and Soviet air forces built few aircraft able to sustain speeds approaching

RIGHT AND INSET: The Europeans also embarked on aircraft development programs of varied success. The SAAB J-35 (inset) was highly successful, but the Dassault Mirage G (right) was perhaps too ambitious and did not enter production. BELOW: The cockpit of the Mirage III fighter belies the late date (1960) of its first deployment.

Mach 3. It did not matter, for air combat continued to be waged in the subsonic and transonic range. The U.S. Air Force deployed the General Dynamics F-111, a variable-sweep fighter-bomber in Vietnam, and the McDonnell Douglas F-15 Eagle, its principal theater-of-operations fighter. The Soviet Air Force built comparable aircraft but not in as great numbers, without as strong a support apparatus (it is estimated that the cost of each F-15 fighter tops $10 billion for the life of the aircraft in terms of support machinery and facilities), and without as sophisticated avionics (electronics).

Paradoxically, the advances that the Soviets showed in the development of supersonic bombers, culminating in the fearsome Tupolev Tu-26, probably one of the fastest bombers ever produced, capable of supersonic flight over relatively short distances. Instead of supersonic speed, the United States developed stealth technology; to use it to create the Northrop B-2 bomber and the Lockheed F-117 fighter, neither of which can match any of the standard bombers in either the American or Russian arsenal for speed (but, as has been pointed out, speed isn't everything); and to toy with satellite anti-

missile programs under the general heading of the Strategic Defense Initiative (SDI or, as the media dubbed it, "Star Wars").

With the collapse of the Soviet Union and the disarray of its aircraft development program, and with stealth technology upsetting the entire global balance of air power, the Advanced Tactical Fighters (ATF) that the United States anticipated it would have to develop to counter improved Soviet fighters may turn out to be unnecessary, and the development of high-speed fighters and bombers may proceed at less than the breakneck speed of the last three decades. Two ATF aircraft have been produced by rival teams, the Lockheed Martin F-22 and the Northrop F-23. Both have produced two prototypes, each fitted with competing engines from General Electric and Pratt & Whitney. Both have unconventional configurations that help provide stealth characteristics. The F-22 won the competition. It has thrust vectoring, which enhances its performance. The Raptor, as it has been named, has supercruise performance, meaning it can fly at supersonic speeds without using its afterburners. As with all modern aircraft, both

OPPOSITE, TOP: The Dassault Mystère IV-N fighter was used by countries without their own fighter production capability. OPPOSITE, BOTTOM: France entered the first rank of fighter producers with the advent of the Mirage 2000. ABOVE: Dassault Mirages lined for assembly. These aircrafts would eventually see extensive usage in the Air Forces of many different countries.

the F-22 and F-23 rely on computers to optimize all parameters of flight.

Two specific aircraft stand out, however, as exemplary models of pushing the envelope of aircraft design: the Lockheed SR-71 Blackbird and the Concorde SST.

THE LOCKHEED SR-71 BLACKBIRD

The amount of misinformation that has been promulgated by the U.S. military (which is understandable and is equaled by the similar campaigns waged by the Soviets and virtually every other nation's military lead-

ership) makes it difficult to say anything authoritative about the Blackbird. President Johnson revealed the existence of the aircraft in 1964 in response to political pressures; otherwise its existence may well have remained a secret for another ten years. The other fact to remember about the Blackbird is that in spite of Lockheed's insistence that the aircraft was developed initially as a next-generation fighter and only later was deployed as a reconnaissance aircraft, the development of this aircraft took place under the auspices of the Central Intelligence Agency and not the U.S. Air Force. The fact that much of the information about the devel-

OPPOSITE AND ABOVE: A defining episode in the most heated stages of the Cold War was the Russian downing of an American U-2 spy plane piloted by Francis Gary Powers, in 1960. BELOW: The U-2 was one of Kelly Johnson's masterpieces and is still considered one of the great achievements of aeronautical design. The U-2 was designed for high-altitude reconnaissance, not for speed. Its downing by a Soviet SA-2 missile led to the development of the much faster SR-71, which could outrun missiles.

opment of the SR-71 (strategic reconnaissance-71) comes from Lockheed publications, some authored by none other than Kelly Johnson, the famed director of Lockheed's Skunk Works facility in Burbank, California, gives ample reason to wonder if the tale bears any resemblance to the facts.

The story told is that the downing of the U-2 spy plane by the Russians in May 1960 and the capture of its pilot, Francis Gary Powers, prompted Kelly Johnson to propose a new aircraft that would be invulnerable to the kind of missile and fighter attack that had dogged the U-2. Originally designated the YF-12 and called a fighter prototype, the plane was enormous for a fighter: 107.5 feet (32.7m) from tip to tail and a wingspan of only 55 feet 7 inches (16.9m). The two engines are mounted in the very short wing and are removed from the fuselage. This was done because the engines are so loud they could quite likely deafen the pilots if placed too close to the cockpit, though this severely cuts down the maneuverability of the plane. In fact, virtually every aspect of this aircraft, from those noted earlier to the fact that a full day of preparation is required by the flight crew in adjusting to the high-percentage oxygen mix they will be breathing in flight, suggests that the SR-71 could never be used as a fighter.

Still, the SR-71 has been a formidable reconnaissance instrument, able to take high-resolution photographs continuously in flight at an altitude of at least 80,000 feet (24,384m) and at speeds exceeding Mach 4. The U.S. Air Force will say only that the SR-71 is able to photograph in detail (good enough to distinguish the make, year, and model of an automobile) an area exceeding 100,000 square miles (259,000 sq km) every hour. With routine flights of five to six hours long, that is indeed a lot of territory. The record acknowledged by the air force (though the plane has almost certainly exceeded these numbers) is a flight in which a speed of 2,070.1 mph (3,330.7kph) was sustained for an extended period at an altitude of 80,257.9 feet (24,462.6m) which took place on May 1, 1965 (the fifth anniversary of the downing of the U-2, which was clearly chosen to convey a political message). The flight was piloted by Robert Stephens and Daniel André.

There are several keys to the performance of the aircraft, and each required many thousands of research hours to develop. The design uses the fuselage itself as the airfoil, though at the higher end of its speed capability the slightest upward tilt of the nose will keep the plane aloft. (The unusual shape of the fuselage is respon

sible for the craft's nickname, "Habu," which is the name of the pit viper found on Okinawa, on which one detachment that flies the SR-71 is based.) The skin of the Blackbird is a top-secret titanium alloy that is able to withstand temperatures of more than 1,000°F (538°C), to which the skin is subject for hours at a time. Virtually every system of the aircraft, from the fuel and hydraulic fluids to the electronic components and wire insulation, has to be designed specifically to endure the long periods of extreme heat that are routinely encountered by the Blackbird in flight.

One very unusual feature of the airplane is that it leaks—on purpose. The Blackbird is constructed so that there is no separate fuel tank within the skin of the plane. The fuselage *is* the fuel tank. The high temperatures reached by the skin cause the metal to expand so much that there are small gaps in the skin that close while the aircraft is in flight. On the ground, however, the fuel seeps out of the airplane and pools. Fortunately the special fuel used by the SR-71 is of very low volatility and does not pose a fire hazard. No aircraft in history has been as far ahead of all competitors as the SR-71, and to this day, no aircraft has ever matched its performance.

During the last three decades of the twentieth century, more than thirty SR-71 Blackbirds have been deployed, at least two of which are double-cockpit instructional versions. There have been at least ten aircraft lost to accidents or scrapped as being mechanically unfixable, some are in service at any time, and

OPPOSITE AND BELOW: If the U-2 represented the ultimate in standard-wing configuration, the SR-71 Blackbird represented the ultimate in the packaging of raw power. One restriction of the Blackbird is that it required extra time aloft after high speed flight to cool down before descending to the lower atmosphere for a landing.

The Concorde SST, seen during takeoff, is undeniably a great achievement in aeronautical design and engineering and is in the eyes of many one of the century's enduring works of industrial art. Had environmental and economic concerns not caught up with it, the aircraft may well have found a central place in modern air transportation.

others are being upgraded and enhanced. Lockheed and the U.S. Air Force have announced the retirement of the Blackbird program a number of times, citing the advent of spy satellites as rendering the SR-71 obsolete, but to this day there are at least two Blackbirds still in service. In the same respect, satellites are expensive, vulnerable, and predictable, so not surprisingly, no SRS—Strategic Reconnaissance Squadron—has ever been ordered to stand down, indicating that cessation of the program has never even been contemplated.

THE CONCORDE SST

The story of the development of the Concorde SST aircraft has been told many times (twice by this author alone!) and is certainly a cautionary tale worth knowing. Its underlying moral is simply stated: there comes a point in the development of a technology when the gains are meager compared with the expenditure of resources. Both the United States and the Soviet Union had made halting forays into the high-risk supersonic transport game—both with disappointing (and in some instances disastrous) results. The eventual building and operation of the Concorde by a British-French consortium serves as a testimony to international cooperation and to the engineering talents of many gifted designers and technicians, on the face of it an excellent example of pushing the envelope to bring supersonic flight to the air traveler. But it is also true that the Concorde is and may well be destined to always be a financial failure, simply because there may not be any compelling reason for people to get anywhere in that much of a hurry. The continued efforts and plans by nations and major aircraft manufacturers to surpass the Concorde with a passenger aircraft capable of supersonic and suborbital flight, many of which are reminiscent of the plans of Norman Bel Geddes to build aircraft the size of ocean liners, give strong indication that some dreams refuse to die, even when they ought to.

The Aerospatiale/British Aerospace Concorde is a remarkable example of international cooperation that set the pattern for many future joint ventures and led directly to the success of the current Aerospatiale series of airliners. The lure of the Concorde concept was the exploitation of the benefits of supersonic speed for travelers. Airliner speeds had not risen appreciably since the introduction of the Boeing 707, which generally cruised at between .74 and .76 Mach. Even today, most airliners

do not cruise at substantially higher speeds. It was believed that businesspeople would find flying the Concorde to be economical, almost without regard to ticket price, simply because of the time it saved them en-route. In the previous history of air transport, a significant advance in speed inevitably brought the customers around. Unfortunately for the Concorde, other problems intervened. The United States, concerned about the environment, did not allow supersonic flight over land, which limited the Concorde to the use of east coast airports. The estimates for the number of Concordes that would be required by major airlines dwindled steadily over time, so that in the end, only Air France and BOAC agreed to purchase the aircraft, and then only as a result of governmental pressures—and subsidies.

None of this detracts from the technical triumph of the Concorde, which carries its passengers in caviar and champagne-laden luxury at Mach 2 speeds. It has had an exemplary safety record to date, and there has been no airliner to challenge it for either speed or prestige. There is no more beautiful sight at an airport than to see the Concorde approach, gleaming white, its nose drooped, its landing gear delicately extended. Three decades after its debut on a twenty-nation sales tour, there is nothing like it in the sky—and there probably never will be.

The next step may well be the hypersonic airliner—but not for many years.

OPPOSITE AND ABOVE: Several design aspects of the Concorde have erroneously been thought to be inspired by aesthetics—like the curve of the wing, which is actually an application of Whitcomb's supercritical wing theory; other aspects have erroneously been thought to be fulfilling an aerodynamic need—like the downward hinge of the cockpit, the main function of which is merely to give the pilot clear visibility of the runway during takeoff and taxiing.

CHAPTER FOUR

OTHER ENVELOPES:
BIGGER, FARTHER, HIGHER, LONGER

WHEN MOST PEOPLE THINK OF AVIATION RECORDS AND PUSHING THE ENVELOPE OF AERONAUTICAL TECHNOLOGY, THEY THINK OF SPEED.

There are, however, other areas where engineering ingenuity has been pushed to the limits in creating magnificent aircraft capable of remarkable feats. This chapter deals with the envelope pushers in four specific areas—aircraft size, flight distance, altitude, and flight duration—and the ongoing efforts to extend the capabilities of aircraft. This chapter also looks at the remarkable renewed efforts to create aircraft powered by solar energy and recent attempts at human-powered aircraft, both of the pedal variety and of ornithopter design. What will become evident (and this should come as no surprise) is that just when it seems an ultimate has been achieved, human ingenuity finds new domains to enter and new achievements to claim.

LEFT: The Boeing 747 is a tribute to the combined will and determination of the Boeing Aircraft Company and the vision of Pan American Airways.

SIZE

During the early stages of serious experimentation in flight, say, in the second half of the nineteenth century, conventional wisdom was that a flying machine would have to be powered by a large steam engine, and that would require a large airfoil and in general a huge design. The invention of the internal combustion engine changed all that, but in the early days, visionaries saw huge machines built to the scale of ocean liners and great ships. In this environment, the notion of a plane like the one the Wright brothers built would have seemed more outrageous than the grandiose designs of dreamer-designers like William Henson and John Stringfellow. It is ironic, therefore, that a machine that may arguably have been the first to fly was, for many years after the December 1903 flights of the Wrights, the largest aircraft on record.

This was the machine built by Hiram Maxim, the expatriated American who was already world-famous as the inventor of the machine gun. Maxim's machine, a 7,000-pound (3,178kg) construction, was powered by two 180-hp engines and had wings 140 feet (42.6m) across. It was mounted on railway tracks 1,800 feet (548.6m) long and was kept grounded by a parallel set of restraining tracks set several inches above the gliders. Observers kept pointing out to Maxim that his machine seemed to be straining against the upper rails and would have taken off given the chance. Maxim, who had a reputation of not being able to take criticism very well, not only refused to eliminate the restraining rails but clipped the wings of the craft to prevent the pesky machine's habit of leaving the underrails. Maxim seems to have been focused on the single problem of determining how much propulsion he could generate with his steam engines. Later reconstructions and models of his machine indicate that Maxim might have been able to add "first to fly" to his list of accomplishments had he not been so stubborn. (However, the flight would not have been controlled. Biographers willing to be gener-

BELOW: Large aircraft design took a leap forward with the building of the Ilya Mourometz, the creation of Igor Sikorsky, seen in this 1915 photo standing on the right on the forward deck.

ous to Maxim believe he was so confounded by the problem of control once an aircraft was airborne that he refused to claim the achievement of first flight until that problem was solved.)

After the Wrights, control became a critical factor in aircraft design, and this placed limitations on the size of aircraft, which makes the achievements of Igor Sikorsky in Russia and at the Gotha aircraft works in Germany during the First World War all the more remarkable. Their aircraft—Sikorsky's *Ilya Mourometz* and the Gotha G-V—were huge aircraft for their day and paved the way for the development of larger aircraft by these nations after the war. The Italians were headed in the same direction, having built large bombers almost from the very beginning of the war. The motivation of the Italians in pursuing this rather expensive line of development puzzled aviation experts at the time. Some believed the driving forces were intentions Italy harbored of establishing military claims on North Africa, and others chalked it up to the ego of Count Gianni Caproni, the foremost airplane manufacturer in Italy

prior to World War II. Caproni built successful large bombers that culminated in the Ca. 42, a triplane with a 98-foot (29.8m) wingspan. This aircraft was dwarfed, however, by what was supposed to be Caproni's masterpiece, the Ca. 60, a plane with nine wings and eight engines. The aircraft crashed in its first test flight over Lake Maggiore, proving an embarrassment to Caproni and marking the end of his development of large planes.

In the cases of both the German and Russian large bombers, the designs were prompted by a recognition by military strategists that huge aircraft would be required for long-range bombing where a front existed between belligerents distant from the centers of population and production. The development of a large bomber has always been an expensive proposition, and it is undertaken only when there is a compelling tactical need for such a weapon. In World War I, Germany and Russia anticipated the need to strike at enemy targets far behind the front lines if a bombing campaign was to be at all effective in influencing the course of the war.

The eight engines of the B-52H strategic bomber hang below and forward of the wing, giving the aircraft an elegant line, but also posing formidable engineering challenges for the builder.

The British did not feel this need. They were fighting a front that was right at their front door. As a result, the Germans and Russians pressed for the development of large long-range bombers early in the conflict; the British did not. In World War II, the Germans depended on establishing control of the areas conquered by the Blitzkrieg and did not see the need for long-range bombers. The same was true for the Japanese. The Allies, however, determined that a bombing campaign against the Germans or the Japanese would, in order to be at all effective, have to be long-range. The oil fields and production plants of the Third Reich were deep in the heart of Europe, and the Japanese seemed to have an unshakable grip on the wall of islands that protected the Japanese mainland.

The American air services, from Billy Mitchell to the present day, believe in the efficacy of the long-range bomber. For many years after World War I, the U.S. Army Air Corps was equipped with biplane bombers, such as the Martin MB-2 or Keystone B-4, whose performance was not significantly greater than the German Gothas of World War I. The first "modern" American bomber was the Boeing YB-9, an all-metal monoplane with retractable landing gear. It was succeeded by the Martin B-10, built to the same formula. However, Boeing led the way into the modern era with its Model 299, which became the famous B-17 Flying Fortress. With it, and the Consolidated B-24 Liberator, the U.S. Army Air Forces conducted a devastating air campaign against Germany. Great Britain's Royal Air Force joined in this campaign with night bombing, using such stellar four-engine aircraft as the Avro Lancaster and the Handley Page Halifax.

The United States had been concerned during the early years of the war that Great Britain would be conquered and not available as a place to station bombers. It therefore embarked upon the development of very long ranged bombers. The first of these to mature was the very best bomber of World War II, the Boeing B-29. Using bases captured in the South Pacific, the B-29s quite literally destroyed Japan with conventional incendiary and high explosive bombs. When the Japanese military still refused to surrender, atomic bombs were dropped on Hiroshima and Nagasaki, ending the war, and forestalling the need for an invasion.

After the war, the other long-range bomber, the Consolidated B-36 Peacemaker, was brought into the inventory, but it was rendered obsolete by the jet age. Boeing produced the B-47, the most important multi-jet aircraft in history, and followed it with the KC-135 tanker and the B-52 bomber. With these three aircraft, the Strategic Air Command became the most powerful military force in history. General Curtiss E. LeMay made the power of SAC known throughout the world and in doing so deterred the Soviet Union from launching a first strike.

A different strategy was followed in the U.S. Air Force development of the Stealth Bomber. An effective Stealth Bomber would require fewer planes and less in the way of fighter and ground support, and would ultimately save money and be more efficient. There was never any doubt about this; what became so controversial was the U.S. Air Force's insistence that it was also necessary to develop the B-1 bomber, a weapon that depended on speed and range, along with the B-2

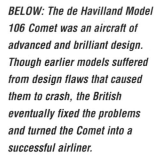

BELOW: The de Havilland Model 106 Comet was an aircraft of advanced and brilliant design. Though earlier models suffered from design flaws that caused them to crash, the British eventually fixed the problems and turned the Comet into a successful airliner.

Stealth Bomber. The deployment, however, of the B-1 in the Persian Gulf, an area where it is inadvisable to risk a B-2 for the policing actions being carried out over Iraq, supports the wisdom of the strategists in developing both planes—decisions that, after all, cost the American taxpayers many billions of dollars.

After the war, the Russians attempted to build on the expertise they had gained in producing large planes and, with the help of an extraordinary popular campaign by Soviet writers and donations from Russian schoolchildren, built the ANT-20, dubbed the *Maxim Gorky*. The *Maxim Gorky* ended its short life in even greater disaster than the Ca. 60. In a May Day 1935 ceremony, in which the Soviets showed off the plane as a propaganda victory, an escort fighter crashed into the

Maxim Gorky, which was destroyed in the ensuing midair explosion. The Russians experienced the same thing again with the crash of the Tu-144, their supersonic transport, in a Paris air show in 1973, as did the British with the crash of their DH 106, a de Havilland Comet, in 1952. These tragedies did not halt aeronautic development in these countries, though development did continue in a different direction. The British, for example, fixed the problems with the Comet and turned it into a successful airliner.

While Russia and England were looking to develop giant land-based aircraft, the United States and Germany were looking toward flying boats as the likeliest venue for attempting to push the size envelope. In Germany's case, the reason was that the provisions of

ABOVE: The flying boats, here the Dornier Wal, were thought to be the way long-distance flying would be done for decades to come. The development of runway construction during World War II, however, made them less attractive for long-distance flying. BELOW: French citizens inspect the remains of the Tupolev 144 supersonic transport after it had crashed in the Paris Air Show in 1973.

the Treaty of Versailles placed severe limitations on the kind of aircraft Germany could develop, but these conditions were relaxed when it came to flying boats. (It was thought that technological know-how gained in the development of flying boats could not be transferred to land-based aircraft because the landing technology lagged so far behind. A flying boat was thought to have limited military utility because it could be rendered unusable by the simple expedient of mining a landing zone.) As for the United States, very little development of large aircraft took place on American soil during World War I, whereas some significant strides were made in the development of naval aircraft. The immigration of Igor Sikorsky to the United States in 1918 increased that area of development; the U.S. and Germany were soon locked in a contest over who could build the biggest flying boat.

Germany, in a sense, won the battle but lost the war: the Dornier Do-X was a flying boat with a wingspan of 157 feet (47.8m) and twelve engines, though their configuration made it appear as if the boat had only six. The Do-X was the lavish and luxurious creation of Claudius Dornier, chief designer for the Zeppelin company. After designing the huge airships that would dominate international travel in the interwar period, Dornier turned his attention to flying boats, bringing to their problems the advanced construction techniques pioneered by Hugo Junkers. It is remarkable to consider that the Do-X, with its cantilevered wings and its powerful 600-hp engines, was airborne in 1929! After a highly publicized world tour, it became clear in 1930 that the plane could not be operated profitably—it was far too heavy and under-

powered to be economically feasible—and Dornier was forced to donate the aircraft to a museum.

The United States was developing smaller but more efficient flying boats. Martin built three M-130s, the most famous of which was the China Clipper. Boeing built twenty Model 314s, one of which became well known as the Yankee Clipper. Neither of these aircraft was as large as the Do-X, but they were the largest aircraft flying during their years of operation and established the viability of large commercial aircraft. As was the case with speed, aircraft manufacturers learned quickly that it was not necessary to be at the cutting edge in order to create a profitable aircraft. In almost every instance, successful air transports were created within the limits set by the larger military aircraft or even earlier commercial enterprises. The dubious financial benefit did not prevent visionaries from attempting to create larger and larger aircraft (it rarely does), and in 1929, industrial designer Norman Bel Geddes assembled a staff of designers to plan a giant flying boat (it was more like a flying pair of luxury liners) that could carry more than one thousand passengers across the Atlantic in first-class opulence. The drawings that have survived from the project, as grand and outlandish as they are, obscure the fact that serious steps were taken, at least at the drafting table, to create the Bel Geddes aircraft, and many of the results of tests and calculations by the designers were valuable to the designers who created the Jumbo Jets of a half century later.

One can count the attempts to actually build larger aircraft than the Do-X on one hand: there were three, possibly four, but no more than five such aircraft. In 1947, Howard Hughes, then yet to gain notoriety as a

RIGHT: British aviation continued developing flying boats after others abandoned them. A Saunders Roe A1 jet-powered flying boat prepares for take-off on the lower Thames in 1951.

reclusive and eccentric millionaire, constructed and briefly flew an immense flying boat, by some accounts the largest aircraft ever built. The record books list the aircraft as the H-4 or the HK-1, but because the aircraft was made mostly of birch plywood, it became universally known as the Spruce Goose. Hughes sank more than $8 million of his own money into the project and piloted the aircraft briefly on November 2, 1947, just 50 feet (15.2m) over the waters of the harbor of Long Beach, California, despite the objections of the Long Beach city authorities. The incident was viewed as an early instance of Hughes' instability, but a closer look reveals that the building of the Spruce Goose was the result of a very serious decision made by the U.S. military, which, at the suggestion of aluminum magnate Henry Kaiser, had asked Hughes to build a giant transport that could evade the German U-boats terrorizing shipping in the North Atlantic and impeding the shipment of war materials to England. The aircraft was assembled in the Hughes Tool Culver City plant, transported to Long Beach by military transport—though the motivation for this aircraft had passed into history, the military was still intensely interested in knowing if a plane of these dimensions was feasible—and fully documented, again by the military. The HK-1, known also by the name *Hercules*, had a wingspan of 320 feet (97.5m)—as long as a football field, including the end zones!—and an overall length of 219 feet (66.7m).

Because it was made of lightweight materials, its weight of 190 tons (172.3t) was little for so massive a craft. By the time Hughes took his creation for its short hop, other aircraft had already demonstrated the feasibility of so large an airplane.

One such giant was the British-built Saro (for Saunders-Roe, the manufacturers) Princess, a commercial flying boat. The Princess was put into commercial use in 1952 and served briefly, mainly as a prestige project for the British. But by the 1950s, a new generation of large airliners had come into service and the days of the flying boat were well past. Nevertheless, because of its brief service as a commercial air transport, a distinction the HK-1 cannot profess, the Saro Princess may lay claim to being one of the largest commercial air transports ever built.

As for land-based aircraft, the Boeing 747 Jumbo Jet, unveiled in February 1969 lays claim to being the largest commercial aircraft ever built—the only dispute arising from what is used as the deciding factor in determining what makes one aircraft "bigger" than another: wingspan, length, seating, capacity, payload, or some formula involving a combination of these factors.

The same dispute arises when one tries to determine the second-largest aircraft ever built (next to the HK-1). The Soviets long claimed that the distinction belonged to the Antonov An-124 Condor; the Americans believed the honor should go to the Lockheed C-5

ABOVE: A cutaway view of the Sikorsky S-42 shows how Pan Am designed the interior along the state room lines of the luxury liners. BELOW: A C-5A transport rolls off the assembly line at the Lockheed Marietta plant in 1967 to become the world's largest aircraft, with a wingspan of nearly 223 feet.

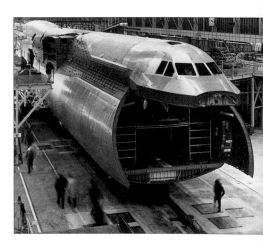

ABOVE AND RIGHT: *The strict safety guidelines and testing that the aviation industry and many governments demanded for both of the most widely used wide-body air transports—the Airbus A300 (above) and the Boeing 747 (right)—are comforting and impressive to anyone flying one of these planes. This has, however, raised questions and concerns about the thoroughness of the safety demands and testing of all aircraft produced up to that point.*

Galaxy. The Condor has a wingspan of 240.5 feet (73.3m), compared with the Galaxy's 222.6-foot (67.8m) wingspan, but the Galaxy is 248 feet (75.5m) long, compared with the Condor's length of 226.6 feet (69m). Since these aircraft were designed to transport personnel and armament, the aviation community (somewhat arbitrarily) decided the issue would be settled by a combination of payload and altitude. In a series of competitive flights conducted in the late 1980s, the Condor outperformed the Galaxy and established a payload-altitude record by taking a payload of 377,473 pounds (171,372.7kg) to an altitude of 35,269 feet (10,750m) on July 26, 1985. An aircraft based closely on the An-124 is the An-224 Mryia Cossack, reputed to be the first aircraft with a gross takeoff weight exceeding 1 million pounds (454,000kg). The United States has, since the 1980s, refrained from participating in head-to-head competition with the Soviet Union in this area for the simple reason that the C-5 series is a principal transport of the U.S. military to trouble spots around the world, and claims of its exact payload and capabilities must remain classified. The Russians, with very little need to ferry soldiers or materials quickly to hot spots around the world until the uprisings in Afghanistan, had little reason to maintain strict secrecy in the An-224's capabilities. Now both nations agree that this information should not be public. In spite of the results of the testing period of the 1980s, however, the aviation community recognizes the continued development of the Galaxy series, and most experts rate the C-5 higher than its Russian counterpart.

SMALL AIRCRAFT

While manufacturers were creating larger and larger aircraft with an eye toward the growing commercial air transportation market, others were trying to build ever smaller aircraft for private and sport use. Because a vast array of small "homebuilt" aircraft has been created over many decades, it is difficult to lay down guidelines that can be used to determine which aircraft is the smallest. The situation is further complicated by the fact that a large number of aircraft skirt the boundary between conventional airplane and autogyro, which combines elements of a helicopter and an airplane. In many aviation record books, however, the record for the smallest aircraft ever produced and flown goes to the *Baby Bird*, a monoplane only 11 feet (3.3m) long, with

The Gee Bee Sportster was a less lethal version of the Gee Bee planes that participated in the Bendix races but was also less maneuverable and less popular among the speedsters.

a wingspan of only 6.25 feet (1.9m) and an empty weight of 252 pounds (114.4kg). The aircraft, built by Don Stits out of wood, steel tubing, and fabric, was flown by Navy pilot Harold Nemer in 1987.

One cannot discuss small aircraft without mentioning the most remarkable small aircraft ever built, the Gee Bee Super Sportster. This aircraft, the product of Zantford "Granny" Granville's imagination and Robert Hall's engineering, dominated the air races of the 1930s and was responsible in large measure for making flying wildly popular during aviation's "golden age" between the world wars. Barely 15 feet (4.5m) long, with a wingspan that varied from 12 to 18 feet (3.6m to 5.4m), depending on the model, the Gee Bee seemed

to all appearances like half an aircraft. That was because it housed a very powerful engine for its diminutive size: a 730-hp Pratt & Whitney T3D1 radial-piston engine. The Gee Bee became celebrated for winning the most important races of the era—the Bendix and the Thompson Trophies, as well as the National Air Races in Cleveland—and it was in a Gee Bee that Major Jimmy Doolittle established the 1932 air speed record of 294.4 mph (473.6kph). The aircraft was reputed to be unstable and it was thought to be the product of the mad designers at the Granville brothers' airplane factory (about whom it was said that they built planes without blueprints, simply making up the specifications as they went along), but in fact the aircraft was the prod-

uct of careful wind tunnel testing by aerodynamicist Alexander Klemin and engineer Howell Miller at New York University.

The Gee Bee was soon discarded, first by Doolittle and then by other racers, as too dangerous to fly, and in fact all models of the Gee Bee ever produced crashed at one time or another, killing a number of pilots. Nevertheless, the Gee Bee's data was used in the production of subsequent aircraft, and another small bundle of power would not be seen for decades.

Unlike the Gee Bee, which killed by accident, the Okha 11 kamikaze bomber killed its pilots on purpose. Launched from a parent plane and with essentially only the ability to rocket-glide to a target with almost no

maneuverability by its pilot, the Okha 11 was about 20 feet (6m) long with a wingspan of just under 17 feet (5.1m). More than 850 of these devilish weapons were built and deployed, and although they were feared, they were ineffective and of little impact on the course of the war in the Pacific.

DISTANCE

In attempting to fly at ever faster speeds, a whole series of technical problems had to be solved if any progress was to be made. Higher speeds required greater propulsion, which required more powerful fuels. It is interesting that while the various developers of jet

One of the few Okha 11 kamikaze aircraft on display shows how little lateral control the pilot had, though some pilots claimed they could alter the course of the aircraft by applying a little "body English." The aircraft proved ineffective as a bomber and served only as a psychological weapon.

engine technology are well known and deservedly lionized for their contributions, little mention is made of those researchers who developed the fuels that made supersonic flight possible. For example, of Jimmy Doolittle's many accomplishments in the field of aviation, he is rarely given credit for spearheading the effort to create 100-plus-octane fuel. (The scant recognition given Doolittle for his efforts in this area, however, is like a ticker tape parade down Broadway compared with the recognition given the true pioneer in the area of aviation fuels, Thomas Midgly. When Midgly is mentioned at all, it is generally as the inventor of Freon, but the Ohio native who directed Dow Chemical for nearly three decades conducted the basic research in the 1920s and 1930s that made 50-plus-octane fuels possible—he developed a custom blend especially for Charles Lindbergh's historic solo flight across the Atlantic—and laid the foundation for all fuel research during World War II and in the postwar period.)

These powerful fuels had their immediate application in the efforts to establish speed and size records, but they also had a direct effect on the distances aircraft could fly without refueling. A more powerful fuel could be used sparingly and yield greater propulsion, so less of it was required for long distances. Along with the more powerful fuels came more efficient and powerful engines, an enterprise that was already well under way since the late nineteenth century for use in land vehicles (automobiles, trucks, and trains) and for electric power generators. Many of the strides made in construction techniques that made larger and lighter aircraft possible were derived from the engineering technology developed for building and bridge construction. In many of the instances of long-distance flying, in which the envelope of what could be accomplished was pushed to new territory, the technology being relied upon by the aviators had been tested in other technological settings or had been adequately bench-tested before anyone climbed into a cockpit—except one: navigation.

The most difficult challenge in long-distance flying, especially in the early years of the route-proving flights before World War II, was simply getting to the destination for which one set out. The standard navigation tools that were available on the surface of the earth were difficult to use in flight aboveground for a variety of reasons. In the first place, an aircraft is generally moving too fast to permit a fix to be made using celestial-navigational

RIGHT AND OPPOSITE: The simple Sperry instrument panel of the early 1920s (right) developed into a complex and sophisticated instrumentation of the flight deck of such aircraft as the Convair 240 (opposite) in the 1950s, marking one way in which post-war aviation electronics and instrumentation were leaps and bounds ahead of earlier industry standards.

tools, and in many instances, long-distance trips are almost certainly going to entail periods when cloud cover makes such measurements impossible. A boat on the sea can cope with this by using a compass to maintain a course, but aviators soon learned that flight entailed other problems that made this difficult and unreliable. Even the most practiced pilot flying through a cloud will easily lose the ability to maintain level flight or detect when he is side-slipping or yawing. Using the ground for dead reckoning also proved unreliable except for the most obvious landmarks, like rivers and cities.

In order to make long-distance flying possible and safe, instruments had to be devised that would give a pilot instant and reliable information on the state of his aircraft as well as similar instant and reliable information on his precise location. This becomes even more pressing as the air becomes more crowded and is particularly important for the execution of a safe landing and takeoff. This was going to require a level of sophistication far beyond the capabilities of electronic equipment in the early decades of the twentieth century (recalling that electronic devices were virtually unknown until the very end of the nineteenth century). The difficulties encountered in navigating, particularly over vast stretches of ocean or uncharted territories of the globe, made the distance flights across the Atlantic and Pacific Oceans, or over the Alps or to

LEFT: An early flight check would take just a few minutes and consisted of little more than making sure the instruments were turned on. BELOW: The many devices later pilots had to constantly monitor made the development of automatic mechanisms that would assist in the flying of the aircraft an absolute necessity.

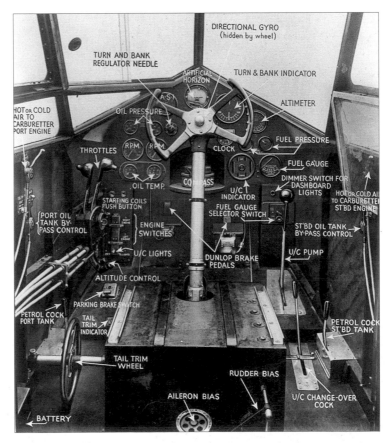

OPPOSITE: *In many ways the*
Spitfire was ahead of its time.
The Spitfire became the symbol
of the Battle of Britain, along
with the Hawker Hurricane.

Australia by way of Africa and southern Asia, so dramatic and dangerous. Even a relatively short hop over the English Channel was fraught with dangers. A minor error of a few fractions of a degree—or a compass misregistering true north because of vibrations or because the aircraft was, contrary to the pilot's sensation, not flying level—could result in missing the coast and finding oneself in the middle of the North Sea or the Atlantic when the fuel ran out. It is believed that most of the more celebrated tragedies that occurred in attempts to cross the Atlantic before Lindbergh were caused not by malfunctioning engines or aircraft, but by errors or failures in navigation.

The solutions to these problems were slow in coming and lagged behind the technology of the rest of aviation. In spite of generous support from the Guggenheim Fund; the application of the extraordinary talents of two gifted instrument engineers, Elmer Sperry and Paul Kollsman; and the assistance of one of the most astute and analytical pilots in aviation history, Jimmy Doolittle, it took a concerted effort of more than eighteen years until a reliable "artificial horizon" instrument was perfected in 1928. The instrument permitted pilots to fly in all but the most inclement weather and led to the development of the gyrocompass, a compass that does not depend on the magnetic North Pole and that operates no matter what the orientation of the aircraft; the rate-of-climb indicator and quick-acting altimeters; bank and yaw indicators; and powerful, lightweight radios that permit communication with the ground and other aircraft. Most important, the gyrocompass permitted the installation of radio beacon detectors for location and navigation.

The extreme difficulty of flying over unmarked terrain or ocean, through clouds, or in the dark of night makes such feats of aerial navigation as Lindbergh's solo flight to Paris in 1927 all the more remarkable. The same may be said of a number of other navigational feats that were even more difficult, such as Georges Chavez crossing the Alps in September 1910; Roland Garros crossing the Mediterranean in September 1913; Luis Candelaria crossing the Andes in April 1918; John Alcock and Arthur Whitten Brown crossing the Atlantic in June 1919; Ernest Hoy crossing the Canadian Rockies in August 1919; Lester J. Maitland and Albert F. Hegenberger's flight from California to Hawaii in June 1927; Bert Hinkler's solo flight from England to Australia in May 1928; Amy Johnson's solo flight over

the same route in May 1930; Jean Batten's faster flight over the same route in May 1934; and Wiley Post's solo flight around the world in July 1933. All these are great examples of airmanship, to be sure, but they could have taken place only as the result of very good (or very lucky) navigation.

The earliest navigation aids consisted of the rather whimsical device of large arrows painted on the tops of barns pointing the way to local airfields. (Comic book aficionados will recall that Superman disguised the giant key to his Fortress of Solitude as a directional arrow.) This was replaced with a system known as radio range, which utilized a simple radio beacon that indicated when an aircraft was outside an approach path or a flight path in the vicinity of an airport. The American approach was to build larger and larger transmitters; not having to deal with borders and other countries sharing its continent (at least from coast to coast), there were no restrictions on the placement of radio towers, as would be encountered in Europe. The system grew into the very-high-frequency omnidirectional radio-range (VOR) network. VOR was used in combination with a second system based on Doppler radar techniques, known as Distance-Measuring Equipment (DME). This system sufficed for American needs until the 1950s, though it did result in crowded air lanes and restricted use of airspace.

The next logical step would be a system of radio beacons that would tell an aircraft where it is, no matter how far from an airport or air installation. Such a system was, in fact, developed by the British during World War II and it permitted RAF aircraft to fly with uncanny accuracy over Germany throughout the war. The system, known simply as Gee, was then developed into one using radio waves with longer wavelengths and thus longer range (LORAN) for use over the ocean and remote regions.

After the war, the British perfected this system even further so that with a minimal number of base stations, aircraft all over the world would be able to determine their locations within several hundred yards. The system, named Decca after the British company that developed it, was considered far ahead of its time and was a clear choice of aviators the world over. However, in 1958, in response to pressure from the United States, the International Civil Aviation Organization (ICAO) decided to make the system then used in the U.S., the combined VOR/DME network, the international standard. At the time, the British accused the ICAO of

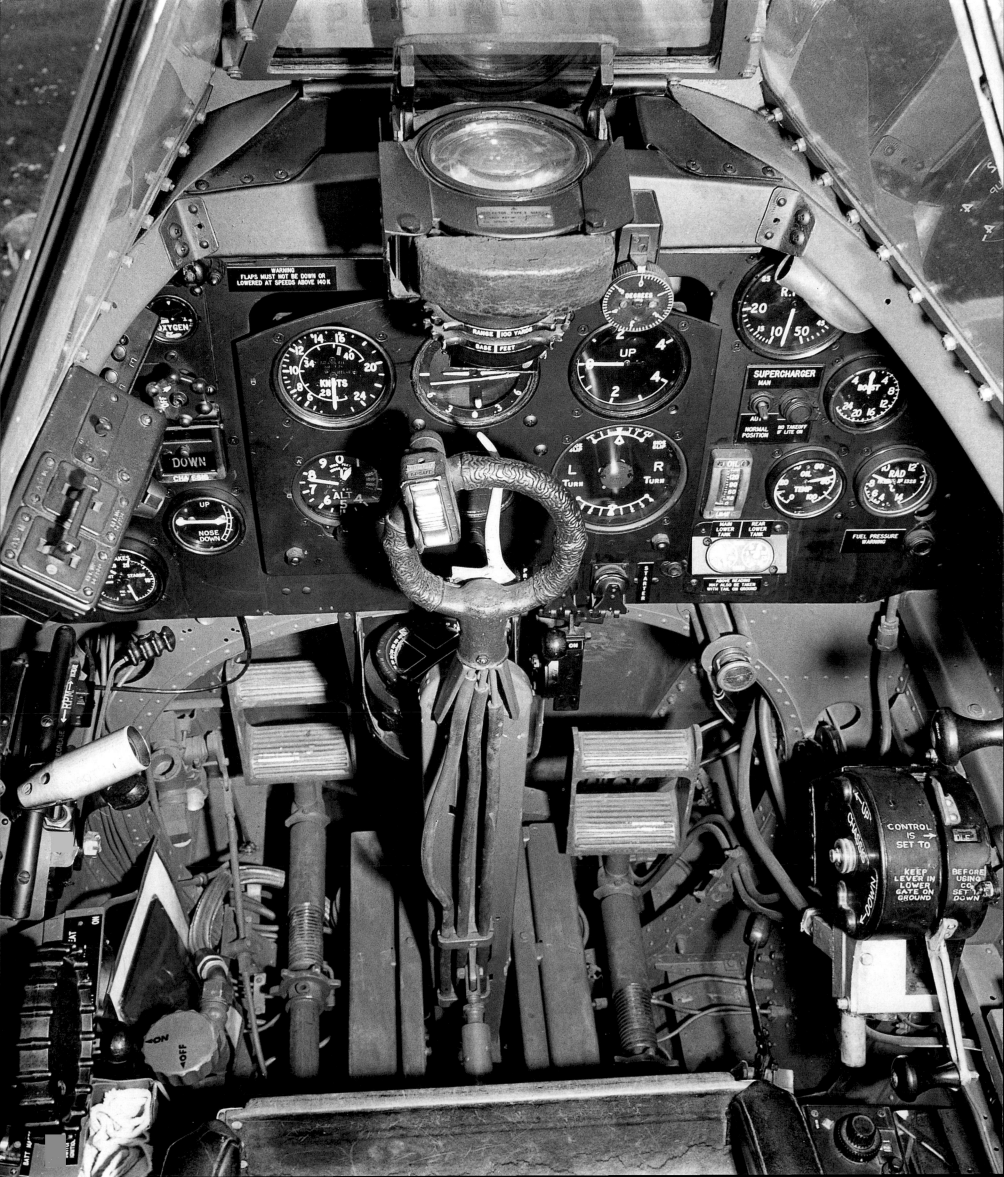

bowing to American political pressure in selecting the inferior system. There is always such intense competition at the international level, for such decisions affect trade for years to come. Today, the globalization of corporations tends to reduce such friction. But a fair assessment of the episode indicates that American interests were not simply motivated by business. (The British did not, after all, have a monopoly on the LORAN technology; they only believed they could do it better than anyone else.)

The ICAO system allowed governments to maintain stricter control over their airspace and proved to be of strategic advantage in several of the small wars in the post–World War II period. It was also true that the United States was developing AWACS technology and anticipated not requiring a LORAN system for military use in the future. The absence of such a system would give the U.S. a tactical advantage in any air war. This point was driven home in 1997 when an American businessman establishing a cellular communication system in Russia was accused of being a spy because he was using satellite location technology routinely used by cellular communication, which could pinpoint a user's location anywhere on the globe to within a few hundred feet. This turned out to be a violation of old Soviet security measures, which prohibited such accurate surveying.

The Russians, it was discovered, had established the same system as the U.S. for the same strategic reasons.

Currently, the navigational systems routinely used by aircraft (and by ships at sea, for that matter) are satellite-based and computer-assisted.

Given all this development of navigational aids, it is easy to conclude that long-distance flying became a snap after World War II, but this is not the case. These devices and systems were effective only over land, and even then only over populated areas of developed countries. In many areas of the world, land-based navigation systems are still not in place, and inertial navigation systems, which permit an aircraft to determine its location without any reference to an outside source, did not become a routine part of aircraft equipment until the early 1970s (so even into the 1960s, Superman's ruse still worked).

As a result of the advances in both aircraft technology and navigation, the FAI has been able to pay even more attention to maintaining distance records after World War II. The 10,000-mile (16,090km) mark was broken in September 1946—with T. O. Davies and E. P. Rankin flying a Lockheed P2V Neptune from Perth, Australia, to Columbus, Ohio, a distance of 11,235.6 miles (18,078km), a remarkable distance for a piston-engine aircraft of the time. Another official FAI record

OPPOSITE AND ABOVE: The integration of pilot acumen and avionic sophistication reached a pinnacle in the F-117 Stealth Fighter. Pilots report that flying the F-117 requires a "suspension of focus" so t hat one is flying by instinct. Paradoxically, it is reported to be a remarkably close approximation of flying "like a bird."

Probably more important—and certainly more dangerous— than his famous distance flights were Wiley Post's altitude flights of 1935, in which he tested and proved the use of pressure suits in high-altitude, long-distance flights.

was entered into the books in January 1962, when a crew commanded by Clyde Evely flew a Boeing B-52H from Okinawa to Madrid, Spain, a distance of 12,532.3 miles (20,164.4km), but many aviation experts believe that record has been broken unofficially many times, both before and since.

The next time the FAI bothered to record a distance milestone was in December 1986, when Dick Rutan and Jeana Yeager (no relation to Chuck Yeager) piloted the *Voyager* in the first (and thus far only) nonstop around-the-world flight. The nine-day flight to and from Edwards Air Force Base in California covered 24,986.66 miles (40,203.5km) and is considered a great feat of not only airmanship on the part of the pilots but of design, by Burt Rutan, Dick's brother, and the various electronics companies that provided lightweight but sophisticated navigation and communications equipment crucial to the flight.

ALTITUDE

As is the case with distance, the altitude envelope has been stretched as a result of a combination of intrepid flying and technological achievement. There are several problems posed by high-altitude flight that began to be tackled in the nineteenth century in connection with balloon flight. At higher altitudes, the pressure of the atmosphere falls progressively. If the pressure at sea level is designated as one hundred atmospheres, then the pressure falls to seventy-five atmospheres at an altitude of 8,000 feet (2,438.4m). Any thinner and a pilot's faculties would be impaired; untrained individuals would have difficulty remaining conscious. The virtual altitude limit for unaided flight should be 10,000 feet (3,048m), at which point relative pressure is sixty-nine atmospheres—except that there are many cases on record of people surviving higher altitudes (pilots are required to use oxygen above 14,000 feet (4,267m) during unpressurized flight). One of the most remarkable records for altitude belongs to Gaston Tissandier, the French captain of the balloon *Zenith*. On April 15, 1875, he and two other aeronauts reached a height of 26,000 feet (7,924.8m), but his companions lost consciousness and died of hypoxia (oxygen deprivation). Only Tissandier, who also lost consciousness, survived. One reason the record is so remarkable is that it was not broken by an airplane until 1919, when Jean Casale flew past the 30,000-foot (9,144m) mark in a Nieuport biplane.

The cruising altitude for commercial aircraft is in the 30,000- to 40,000-foot (9,144 to 12,192m) range, and for supersonic aircraft it is in the 40,000- to 60,000-foot (12,192 to 18,288m) range. This means that special equipment is required for most kinds of commercial aviation, and even more serious measures are necessary for the higher altitudes attained by military aircraft. The oxygen content of the air breathed is adjustable; for example, at 33,000 feet (10,058.4m), a 100-percent-oxygen air content delivers the equivalent of normal breathing at sea level (where oxygen comprises only one-fifth of the air content). Balloon flight in the nineteenth century had prepared aviators for this adjustment—even Tissandier had experimented with rubber containers of pure oxygen on his historic flight—and by the second decade of aviation, fliers intending to make high-altitude flights knew that they required richer oxygen blends of air to breathe. (Tissandier had also discovered that one of the effects of hypoxia is diminished judgment, so it is impossible for someone suffering from it to know that he is in danger. Tissandier's companions were unable to discern the need to breathe from their oxygen-rich containers until it was too late.) But another effect of high-altitude flight had not been recognized until airplanes: decompression sickness, or the aeronautical equivalent of the bends. The slow ascent and descent of balloons gives the body time to decompress and adjust to the change in altitude, but this is not the case with airplanes.

Decompression sickness occurs because nitrogen pressure in the blood and in body tissue does not adjust as quickly as the more soluble oxygen and carbon dioxide, so as the pressure changes rapidly, bubbles of nitrogen appear in blood and in body tissue (like bubbles of carbon dioxide in soda water). A bubble in the blood can cause a hemorrhage, a blood clot, or heart failure, and gaseous bubbles in tissue can cause paralysis or even death. This problem was discovered in the late 1920s and became a serious problem during World War II, when bomber pilots experienced bendslike symptoms after flights in which they ascended quickly to lower pressure altitudes The prewar solution to this problem was to allow pilots to breathe pure oxygen mixtures for an hour before and an hour after the flight (and, of course, during the flight), a technique that flushes nitrogen out of the system until a pressure equilibrium can be reached. Breathing pure oxygen presents problems of its own, however, and it was clear that the only real solution was going to be pressurization, that is, creating an atmosphere in the passenger cabin, or in the immediate vicinity of the flier, that approximated ground conditions.

The pioneer in the use of pressurized suits for high-altitude flight was none other than Wiley Post. Though Post never set an altitude record (his main motivation was to fly high enough to catch the jet stream and improve his speed), his 1935 flights using a pressurized suit that looked more like an underwater diver's outfit paved the way for other high-altitude fliers. Over the next fifteen years, the FAI recorded a succession of flights that broke the 40,000-, 50,000-, and 60,000-foot (12,192, 15,240, and 18,288m) marks by 1953, the last in May of that year by Walter F. Gibb, flying an Electra; and then the 70,000- and 90,000-foot (21,336 and 27,432m) marks were broken, the latter in May 1958 by Howard Johnson, flying a Lockheed F-104-A.

The advent of manned space flight (and the high level of secrecy that accompanies the flights of high-altitude reconnaissance aircraft) has pretty much done away with altitude records in the popular mind, but not in the minds of aviation experts and enthusiasts, who maintain an interest in high-altitude flight for both balloons and air-breathing (prop- or jet-driven) aircraft. In 1959 and 1960, realizing that the publicity value of such records would soon diminish in the wake of manned space flight, the United States and the Soviet Union made concerted efforts to establish altitude records. In December 1959, Joe J. Jordan piloted an F-104-A past the 100,000-foot (30,480m) mark, but in April 1961, Georgiy Mosolov took a MiG E-66-A to 113,890 feet (34,713.6m). The current record for the highest altitude attained by an air breathing plane as ratified by the FAI is held by Alexander Fedotov, who piloted a Mikoyan Ye-266M on August 31, 1977, to a height of 123,524 feet (37,650.1m)—where 99.9 percent of the earth's atmosphere was beneath him. This

BELOW: The flight suit of a pilot of an F-104 fighter is as vital a piece of equipment as anything on the plane itself. The partial pressure suit worn by this pilot will inflate if the cockpit suffers a sudden decompression. PAGES 132–133: The exact performance capabilities of the F-117 Stealth Fighter remain classified. F-117s flew hundreds of precision bombing missions during the Persian Gulf War.

altitude is almost 10,000 feet (3,048m) higher than the official altitude for the highest manned flight in a balloon, held by V.A. Prather. The unofficial record for balloon altitude is held by Nicholas Piantanid, who reached an altitude of 123,800 feet (37,734.2m) in a February 1, 1966, ascent from Sioux Falls, South Dakota. The record is unofficial because Piantanid lost his life during the flight, though the fatality probably occurred during the descent after the record was set.

DURATION

The flight of the *Voyager*, which lasted nine days, three minutes, and forty-four seconds, not only marked the first nonstop circumnavigation of the globe by an aircraft but also set the duration record for an unrefueled aircraft flight. Duration records became obsolete shortly before World War II, when the development of two technologies made it possible for aircraft to remain aloft virtually indefinitely: the autopilot and midair refueling. The difficulty in maintaining trim for an aircraft in flight (that is, keeping all the forces in balance so that the plane continues in uniform flight) was considered a real obstacle to flights of long duration. Pilots know that flying an aircraft is so much more complex an operation than, say, driving an automobile that no automatic pilot system can ever be totally entrusted with the control of an aircraft. Yet the fatigue that a pilot would experience in maintaining control of an aircraft for long periods would virtually ensure an eventual loss of control, with ensuing catastrophic consequences.

The effort to create a system that would accompany the pilot or even replace pilot control for some period began as early as 1912, with Elmer Sperry working with the ingenious Glenn Curtiss. A major step in this direction was the series of "blind" flights sponsored by the Guggenheim Fund and conducted by Jimmy Doolittle using equipment he and Sperry had developed. In the blind flight of September 24, 1929, a hood was placed over the cockpit and the aircraft took off, conducted air maneuvers, and landed; it demonstrated once and for all the effectiveness of instrument flying. A totally reliable automatic pilot system was not in place, however, until the late 1930s. Sperry's system of very sensitive yet durable and reliable gyroscopes alleviated the strain of constantly maintaining control of the aircraft in flight and allowed pilots to reorient themselves.

The F-104 Starfighter, described by pilots as "a missile with a man it it," has proven to be both a remarkable aircraft and a dangerously unmanageable one; the Germans dubbed it "the widowmaker." However, it has been deemed suitable for attempts at establishing new records by the U.S. Air Force and has been a favorite of test pilots for several decades.

Midair refueling systems developed faster and were routinely used for long-distance flights in the 1920s, since it was sometimes easier and safer to refuel in the air. Midair refueling was made a standard operational procedure by the Strategic Air Command and other air forces, but has not been used by commercial operators.

The team that set a duration record for the longest flight by a light aircraft utilized yet another strategy to avoid landing to refuel—using a hook, they picked up fuel and food from a truck speeding underneath the plane. The record-setting flight was made in 1959 by Robert Timm and John Cook, who flew a Cessna 172 Hacienda for sixty-four days, twenty-two hours, nineteen minutes, and five seconds, taking off from McCarren Airfield in Las Vegas, Nevada, on December 4, 1958, and landing at the same airfield on February 7, 1959; few aviators have set their sights on breaking it.

The advent of solar-powered drone aircraft, currently in use for weather observation and reconnaissance, and nuclear-powered aircraft, with which the U.S. Air Force experimented in the 1960s, makes it possible for an airplane to remain aloft indefinitely.

BELOW: Midair refueling has become so commonplace in military aviation that it is accepted as a routine part of even record-setting flights. LEFT: Dick Rutan and Jeana Yeager co-pilot their Long EZ before their round-the-world Voyager flight. LEFT, INSET: The Rutan Voyager which made its historic flight in 1986. One of the most important elements of the plane's design was the rear stabilizer mechanism (the twin tall tail assemblies in the rear) designed to control yaw. The pilots' position in the plane severely cut down their reaction time to destabilizing motions of the plane, so the aircraft itself had to compensate.

CHAPTER FIVE

THE FUTURE OF ENVELOPE PUSHING

THE NOTION THAT THE PERIOD OF INTENSE INNOVATION IN THE DESIGN OF AIRCRAFT IS OVER, THAT THE ODD DESIGNS OF THE EARLY YEARS OF FLIGHT HAVE GIVEN WAY TO THE SENSIBLE AND TESTED CONFIGURATIONS

and systems developed by aircraft manufacturers through the middle decades of the twentieth century so that pushing the envelope in the 1990s and in the early twenty-first century means developing better versions of these tried-and-true designs, is as outmoded and absurd as the belief (held seriously in some quarters) that science is at an end and that all that remains is chasing down the last decimal and clearing up a few pesky problems. Both stances wreak of hubris and smack of the arrogance of fin de siècle science, when the same things were said—of both flight and science—only to have both worlds turned on their heads at the very start of the new century.

This point was brought home recently with the death of celebrated entertainer John Denver, who died in a plane crash in 1997 while flying what was described as "an experimental aircraft." The news media watched carefully as drug tests were performed on

LEFT: Flight offers the mechanically inclined the opportunity to experiment and tinker as does no other form of transportation. The "homebuilt" small seaplane shown here might have been built at any time during the past fifty years and might be expected to have an active life of decades.

BELOW AND OPPOSITE: Canard configurations—in which the larger wing providing lift is in the rear and the smaller elevator wing is in the front—are particularly favored by private small plane builders. This configuration not only provides a better view from the pilot's seat, it offers a greater sense of control. It also requires a greater degree of piloting skill.

Denver to determine if the crash was caused by any drug-induced impairment on the part of the famous singer, the implication being that this was the only possible explanation. Only when it was determined that drugs were not involved did newspeople ask the question: what might have caused the crash and just exactly what was "experimental" about Mr. Denver's aircraft? The public was stunned to learn that the number of experimental aircraft, which have to be licensed and certified as airworthy by the FAA and are currently being flown and tested, number more than two thousand. Tinkering, it would seem, is alive and well in private airplane hangars, garages, and workshops across the country.

Many of the innovative designs one encounters on the Web (and in the sky) are either solar-powered aircraft or aircraft powered by the pilot, bringing to life the age-old dream of flying by one's own power. The power output of such aircraft is stingy in the extreme, so aeronautical designers were called on to create aircraft much more efficient aerodynamically than anything envisioned in the entire history of aviation. Two designers showed the way in these fields and their designs have been the basis for the most important work. One is Burt Rutan, designer of the *Voyager*, in which his brother, Dick, and Jeana Yeager

flew nonstop around the world; the other is Dr. Paul B. MacCready, designer of the *Gossamer Albatross*, the human-powered aircraft that crossed the English Channel in 1979. Both men had long experience in soaring (i.e., unpowered gliding), which they brought to bear in the designing of their landmark aircraft, much the same way German designers, forced to experiment with unpowered gliders by the provisions of the Treaty of Versailles after World War I, developed advanced aerodynamic designs by virtue of their handicap.

Human-powered flight—or, more accurately, the dream of human-powered flight—has a long history, predating the advent of the steam or internal combustion engine. The late-nineteenth-century glider pioneer Otto Lilienthal believed it was possible to create a wing configuration that would enable a person to take off from a standing position and fly, provided there was a wind. (Before dismissing Lilienthal, recall that the Wrights conducted their experiments at Kitty Hawk because of the strong Carolina winds, and that their first flight might not have taken place if the air had been dead calm that December day in 1903.) Lilienthal experimented with such elaborate configurations and was preparing to attach an engine to the wings when he died in a crash as a result of a stall. Once the Wrights demonstrated the effectiveness of the internal combustion engine in aviation, interest in human-powered flight evaporated.

In the 1930s and 1940s, interest was rekindled when a engineering group in Frankfurt offered a prize in 1933 for the first human-powered flight of an aircraft around two markers 1,640 feet (500m) apart. Similar prizes were offered in Italy and the Soviet Union at about the same time; none of them was ever claimed. In 1935, two engineers at the Junkers Company claimed to have flown a human-powered aircraft, the *Mufli*; Enea Bossi, an Italian designer, flew a twin-propeller human-powered aircraft, the *Pedaliante*, in 1937. But both flights were considered more glides than actual flights insofar as they involved a launching from a height or by a catapult.

Then, in 1959, British industrialist Henry Kremer offered a prize of £5,000 for the first human-powered flight that could fly a figure eight around two markers about a half mile (800m) apart, or roughly the same maneuverability of the early Wright *Flyer*. During the next eighteen years, several unsuccessful attempts were made and the prize was increased by Kremer, in stages, to £50,000, until the feat was accomplished on August 23, 1977, by Bryan Allen, flying the *Gossamer Condor*, an aircraft designed by Paul B. MacCready. The flight

By the time the Daedalus was built, a great deal had been learned about the mechanics of human-powered flight, which would find applications to flight powered by any comparatively low-energy source, such as solar power.

took place in Shafter, California, and lasted all of seven minutes and twenty-seven and a half seconds. (The *Gossamer Condor* now hangs in the Smithsonian Air and Space Museum.)

MacCready's design introduced the semirecumbent cyclist position for the pilot and, ironically, used a means of control known as wing-warping first used by the Wright brothers. (Ailerons required equipment that made the craft too heavy.) The design allowed a well-conditioned cyclist (which Allen was) to put out four hundred watts of power for long periods of time. In spite of this, Allen was on the verge of exhaustion at the end of the flight.

Remembering that it was Louis Blériot's flight across the English Channel in 1909 that sparked aviation in the early years of the twentieth century, Kremer offered a prize of £100,000 for the first human-powered flight across the channel. MacCready's team developed the *Condor* into the *Gossamer Albatross* and claimed the Kremer prize, again with Allen in the cockpit, crossing the channel on June 12, 1979. The flight from Folkestone, Kent, in England to Cap Griz Nez in France into a strong head wind was a difficult one; several times Allen thought of ditching the craft, and when he landed, the plastic cockpit was fogged with the steam being produced by his straining body. The time of the flight, two hours and forty-nine minutes, was a full hour longer than anticipated. It established an endurance record and a distance record for human-powered flight of 22.26 miles (35.8km). This record was broken by a group of students from MIT, who flew their *Light Eagle* over Edwards Air Force Base 36.45 miles (58.6km) in a closed circuit on January 22, 1987, with Glenn Tremml at the controls.

Much to Kremer's dismay, all this activity did little to stimulate research in the field, so he offered yet another prize in 1983, this time for speed: £20,000 for the first human-powered flight to cover a 4,921-foot (1,500m) course in less than three minutes. After an intense race between MacCready's team and the MIT group, the prize was taken by the upstart MIT students flying the *Monarch B*. Kremer established a whole series of prizes: £50,000 for the first human-powered aircraft to fly a winding course of 25 miles (40.5km); another £50,000 for a human-powered aircraft that could fly in winds of more than 10 mph (16kph) instead of the near calm that current designs require. Many of the prizes are still unclaimed. The race and Kremer's financial incen-tives have, however, stimulated research in the area, and there are currently more than one hundred programs, each with several prototypes registered, in active pursuit of one record or another.

Many of the MIT students involved in the *Monarch B* project became part of the *Daedalus* project under the auspices of United Technologies and under the leadership of Steven Bussolari. The *Daedalus* team realized that the challenge of human-powered flight was two-pronged: they would need to create a very light-weight and efficient aircraft, but also develop a means of delivering sufficient nutrients to the power source—the human being—to prevent fatigue in long flights. Following extensive testing of cockpit designs and liquid nutrients, the *Daedalus* flew from the island of Crete to Santorini Island, the course traced by the Daedalus of ancient myth, establishing the straight-line record for human-powered flight of 74 miles (119km) on April 23, 1988. The aircraft was piloted by cyclist Kanellos Kanellopoulos, who showed no signs of fatigue at the end of the flight. Unfortunately, a broken wing forced him to end the flight in the waters off Santorini just 33 feet [10m] short of his destination.

All of these human-powered flights have taken place at very low altitudes; the *Daedalus* rarely flies higher than 33 feet (10m) above the ground. Intense research is under way on both sides of the Atlantic to create human-powered aircraft that will fly higher, longer, far-ther, and faster. One such aircraft, the *Raven*, is being developed by the Boeing Company. With a wingspan of 115 feet (35m) but weighing only 75 pounds (34kg) (or, as the company reports, about the weight of all the pillows carried on a Boeing 747), this human-powered aircraft is able to maintain extended flight with only three hundred watts of power; at four hundred watts it may be able to exceed heights of 1,000 feet (304.8m) for brief periods.

Meanwhile, an important area of research for the MacCready team and for his company, AeroVironment, remains the application of what is learned in the area of human-powered aircraft to solar-powered aircraft. MacCready's *Solar Challenger*, an aircraft similar in design to the *Gossamer Albatross* but with more than six-teen thousand solar cells on the upper surface of the wings, performed the first purely solar-powered test flight on November 20, 1980. The qualification "pure" is added because an earlier flight in 1978 was claimed as

PAGES 146–147: A Pietenpol Aircamper biplane surveys the landscape. The biplane is highly dependent upon its wires and struts. Removing any of them would literally cause the plane to fall apart.

the first flight by a solar-powered aircraft, but most engineers regarded the aircraft, the *Solar One*, a hybrid because it used electric storage cells that collected solar energy and then powered the propellers. Still, the *Solar One* did pave the way for MacCready's crowning achievement, the *Pathfinder*, an unmanned solar-powered aircraft capable of reaching very high altitudes and staying aloft for very, very long periods. The *Pathfinder* can achieve altitudes of more than 100,000 feet (30,480m) and fly in the stratosphere virtually continuously, powered by solar energy during the day and battery power at night. (For this reason, the *Pathfinder* is sometimes referred to as "the poor man's satellite.")

...AND EVEN NOISIER WAYS

Periodically, the large aircraft manufacturers unveil a plan for a very large aircraft that will carry huge cargoes or many passengers long distances, and it is clear to nearly everyone that this is done mainly for the publicity. Occasionally, however, one of these plans, because it incorporates a technological breakthrough or addresses an overwhelming demand in the marketplace, takes on a life of its own and races toward practical development. Such a project is the "space plane," a proposed aircraft that can take off and achieve suborbital altitudes and

speeds that make it possible for passengers to fly to the Pacific rim countries from North America and Europe in four to five hours.

There are three technologies that must be fully developed to make this dream a reality, though even if it became technically feasible, it is difficult to see why enough people would be in that much of a hurry to get to the other side of the globe. Two of the technologies—lifting body aerodynamics and aerospike rocket propulsion—are practically as far along as they need to be in order to start taking this possibility seriously; the third—metallic thermal protection—is progressing quickly, driven by the sense that a completely reusable single-stage-to-orbit vehicle (SSTO), the fulfillment of a long-held dream of aerospace engineers and planners, may see the light of day in our lifetime.

The first technology involves the creation of a narrow-body airfoil that provides lift by virtue of its design and dispenses with the use of wings. This design has the advantage of eliminating the leading edge of wings, which become the hottest parts of the aircraft as it reenters the atmosphere. The aerodynamics of wingless aircraft, kept aloft by the lift provided by the shape of the fuselage itself, was worked out in the X-25 project carried out in the 1960s and early 1970s by Martin-Marietta. Many of these findings were used in the design

BELOW AND RIGHT: The 1990s have seen a spurt in innovative designs and enthusiastic interest in experimental aircraft. Homebuilts like the Glasair (below) incorporate design innovations developed for the space program and for eventual use in the X-33, a suborbital commercial aircraft, an artist's rendition of which is shown here (right).

of the Space Shuttle, which relies more on its fuselage shape for aerodynamic lift than on its wings, which provide control surfaces for the vehicle's reentry and landing glide. The immense heat on the underside of the Space Shuttle is borne by the craft's famous heat-resistant ceramic tiles, but ceramic tiles cannot be bolted to the metal fuselage and they cannot be made very large. As a result, they are glued to the underside of the craft, and some of the tiles come loose and are lost routinely in virtually every Space Shuttle landing. Creating heat-dissipating tiles made out of titanium metal would increase the safety of an SSTO immensely, and such tiles have been developed and tested successfully by NASA.

Of course, a more controlled rocket propulsion system—one that could burn longer and at lower power but still provide the thrust necessary to achieve the kinds of speed and altitude required for suborbital flight—would go a long way toward solving this problem. Such a system has been developed by Rocketdyne in California and has been successfully tested in a long series of tests beginning in the late 1970s. The system, known as the aerospike system, amounts to simply configuring the exhausts of the rocket engine to allow maximum efficiency depending on the needs of the flight at different phases. The trick has been to develop alloys capable of withstanding very high temperatures since it is these alloys that shape the rocket exhaust. The test program for this project is known as the X-33, and the name given to the vehicle it will eventually spawn is *VentureStar*. The combination of these three technologies will allow *VentureStar* to travel the critical distance between 25 and 50 miles (40.2 and 80.4km) up—the heights at which the Space Shuttle experiences its maximum thermal and aerodynamic stress, making it the most dangerous part of the flight—in twice the time; the slower descent will result in lower skin temperatures and a safer reentry. NASA planners believe *VentureStar*, or a vehicle very much like it, will become operational in the twenty-first century, though at the current state of technology such a program would dwarf the Space Shuttle program in cost.

Manufacturers also realize that the safety standard of such vehicles must be much higher than it is for conventional aircraft, since a relatively minor problem in a 747 could be catastrophic 50 miles (80.4km) above the surface of the earth. Ultimately, it may turn out that passenger comfort and safety are the chief obstacles to pushing the envelope of aviation to the SSTO.

LEFT: Suborbital vehicles such as the OSC/Rockwell X-34, a concept of which is shown, are being designed to be able to propel satellites into space in addition to whisking people and goods around the globe, thus giving them more economic viability than a plane used for passengers alone.

LOOKING BEYOND THE FUTURE

It should be clear at this point that the period of experimentation, tinkering, and exploring the unknown, all part of the enterprise referred to as pushing the envelope, is anything but over or dormant. Just as the earliest glimmer of hope in the history of aviation was in the form of toys—kites or the hand-spun propeller that was launched like a helicopter by children in the eighteenth century—it is also the case that the many paper airplane contests held in many parts of the world continually produce novel designs and configurations that defy explanation and baffle aerodynamicists. It is certainly possible that one or several of these designs will find applications in the needs of aviation and become the basis of an entirely new area of aviation. Jack Northrop's flying wing design has been resurrected to become the basis for the design of the Stealth Bomber, so anything is possible.

I end this narrative with the following anecdote. In the late 1960s, I was privileged to attend a lecture by eminent physicist and futurist Freeman Dyson about the design for a spacecraft capable of reaching speeds of nearly (say, more than 80 percent of) the speed of light. For three hours the audience listened to Dyson's conjectures and followed his calculations, and it seemed that he had devised a design that could accomplish its goal of very high speed space flight. Professor Dyson then calculated the cost of this vehicle—and it turned out to cost, at a minimum, thirty times the gross national product of the United States. The assembled left with the feeling that human civilization was going to have to progress quite a bit in terms of harnessing its resources and its population and directing them in the creation of wealth for quite some time before anyone boarded Professor Dyson's rocket ship. Ultimately, it is likely to be the mundane matters of national development and economics, and not barriers of imagination or ingenuity, that will determine how far humankind will push the envelope of flight—or any other field.

LEFT AND ABOVE: We have become so accustomed to flight that the marvel of flying in something like the F-15 Eagle fighter aircraft seems a routine part of the military. Yet fighter pilots overwhelmingly come from the ranks of men and women intoxicated more by the thrill of flight than by the lethal weaponry of the machine.

BIBLIOGRAPHY

Readers are referred to the bibliography that appeared in the first book in this series, *Conquer the Sky*, in which fifty of the most outstanding titles covering the full range of subjects in the history of aviation were described and organized. Here, the focus is on works dealing with the cutting edge of experimentation and the ongoing efforts of designers, manufacturers, and pilots to push the envelope of flight. What is now true but was not a scant three years ago is that the largest single source on innovative aviation and the history of pushing the envelope is the Internet, with some fifty Web sites on related subjects, growing virtually every week.

GENERAL

Anderson, John D. *History of Aerodynamics*. Cambridge University Press, 1997. The capstone to an illustrious career as an aviation historian and a master teacher. Its most interesting aspect is the way it points to a future for the science and how much there is yet to learn.

Hallion, Richard. *Designers and Test Pilots*. Time-Life, 1983. A volume in the *Epic of Flight* series but a cut above the rest. The one volume in the series every enthusiast must have above all others.

Myrabo, Leik, and Dean Ing. *The Future of Flight*. Pocket Books, 1985. Though a bit dated, this book offers an interesting perspective on how aviation is likely to proceed into the next century.

CHAPTER ONE

Gray, George W. *Frontiers of Flight: The Story of NACA Research*. Knopf, 1948. An interesting account of the role that institutional and financial support played in the growth of aviation into the supersonic realm.

Gruenhagen, Robert. *Mustang*. ARCO, 1969; and Morgan, Len. *The P-51 Mustang*. ARCO: 1963. If I take a beating for anything in this book, it will surely be for the conclusions drawn about the role of the Mustang in the breaking of the sound barrier. I defer to these two books, though I admit to wishing I were on more solid ground.

Miller, Ronald E., and David Sawers. *The Technical Development of Modern Aviation*. Routledge & Kegan Paul, 1968. One of the few histories that focuses on the step-by-step development of systems that permitted the headline-grabbing feats of aviators.

CHAPTER TWO

Burnet, Charles. *Three Centuries to Concorde*. Mechanical Engineering Press, 1979. Places the development of the SST in historical context as no other book on the subject has. After reading this, one comes away almost believing the SST has a future.

Sabbagh, Karl. *Twenty-First Century Jet: The Making and Marketing of the Boeing 777*. Scribner, 1996. In the hands of Sabbagh, the entire history of aviation and the design of commercial aircraft come together in a mad blend of science, business, government, and hucksterism. A book that says as much about the current state of technology as it does about the state of aeronautical development.

Wilson, George C. Flying the Edge: *The Making of Navy Test Pilots*. Naval Institute Press, 1992. Along with books on the same subject by Richard Hallion and Tom Wolfe, this is a marvelous look at a breed apart and the intense world of experimental aeronautics.

CHAPTER THREE

Hallion, Richard P. *Supersonic Flight: Breaking the Sound Barrier and Beyond*. Brassey's, 1997. This reissue of a 1972 classic contains revisions and additional material that make this a welcome publication. Hallion is accurate and compelling, and never compromises on either the technical details or the human drama.

Reithmaier, Larry. *Mach 1 and Beyond: The Illustrated Guide to High-Speed Flight*. Tab, 1995. A thorough summary that does not stint on the aerodynamics of supersonic flight.

Rotundo, Louis. *Into the Unknown: The X-1 Story*. Smithsonian Institution Press, 1994. A very readable and interesting take, with a plausible account of the reality (such as it was) of the sound barrier. Compare this story with the one told by Henry Matthews of the Soviet supersonic flight project in Samolyot 346: *The Untold Story of the Most Secret Postwar Soviet X-Plane* (HSM, 1996), in which a profound disrespect for the problems of supersonic flight created many problems for the Russian program.

CHAPTER FOUR

Mohler, Stanley R., and Bobby H. Johnson. *Wiley Post, His Winnie Mae, and the World's First Pressure Suit*. Smithsonian Institution Press, 1971. A fascinating account about a forgotten episode of one of the greats in aviation history, though the book is very hard to find.

Wolko, Howard S. *In the Cause of Flight: Technologists of Aeronautics and Astronautics*. Smithsonian Institution Press, 1981. An endlessly fascinating account of what aeronautical research is really like by one of the most talented aviation writers of recent times—and one of aviation literature's best-kept secrets.

Yeager, Jeana, Dick Rutan, and Phil Patton. *Voyager*. Knopf, 1990. A journeymanlike telling of the historic flight, but with not enough material by or about Burt Rutan, the aircraft's designer. The flight certainly was a great feat of airmanship, but it was also the aircraft's brilliant design that made it all possible. For more on the design (but less on the flight), see Vera Foster Rollo's *Burt Rutan: Reinventing the Airplane* (Maryland Historical Press, 1991).

CHAPTER FIVE

Dwiggins, Don. *Man-Powered Aircraft*. Tab, 1979. Not as gripping a tale as Grosser's (see below), but clearer on many technical points (on which Grosser seems to have been reluctant to elaborate).

Grosser, Morton. *Gossamer Odyssey: The Triumph of Human-Powered Flight*. Houghton-Mifflin, 1991. The detailed account of the making and flying of the *Gossamer Albatross* by a member of the design team, with a wonderfully detailed history of human-powered flight as a bonus. Available as a well-illustrated Dover paperback.

Nadel, Ethan R., and Steven R. Bussolari. *American Scientist*, vol. 76, no. 4 (July-August 19xx). A detailed account of the flight of the *Daedalus*, complete with a description of all the scientific research behind the flight. Bussolari was director of flight operations for the project.

Siuru, Busick, and Siuru. *Future Flight: The Next Generation of Aircraft Technology*. Tab, 1994. Strongly emphasizes the big suborbital aircraft, which are bound to become a reality, more or less, sooner or later.

The Russian MiG-15 soared in the skies above Korea during the 1950s, pitted against American fighters.

INDEX